THE OLD GREY WHISTLE TEST
QUIZ BOOK

MARK PAYTRESS

Foreword by
ANDY KERSHAW

BOOKS

1 3 5 7 9 10 8 6 4 2

Published in 2012 by BBC Books, an imprint of Ebury Publishing
A Random House Group company

Main text by Mark Paytress
Copyright © Woodlands Books Ltd 2012
Foreword © Andy Kershaw 2012

The Random House Group Limited Reg. 954009

Addresses for companies within the Random House Group can be
found at www.randomhouse.co.uk

A CIP catalogue record for this book is available from the British
Library

ISBN 978 1 84990 502 2

The Random House Group Limited supports the Forest
Stewardship Council (FSC®), the leading international forest
certification organisation. Our books carrying the FSC label are
printed on FSC® certified paper. FSC is the only forest certification
scheme endorsed by the leading environmental organisations,
including Greenpeace. Our paper procurement policy can be found
at www.randomhouse.co.uk/environment

Commissioning editor: Albert DePetrillo
In-house editor: Joe Cottington
Project editor: Steve Tribe
Proofreader: Kari Speers
Additional fact checker: Andy Neill
Production: Phil Spencer

Printed and bound in Great Britain by Clays Ltd, St Ives PLC

To buy books by your favourite authors and register for offers,
visit www.randomhouse.co.uk

CONTENTS

WHISTLE TEST
APPRECIATION

When I was thirteen, I accidentally strayed into a parallel universe. Alone, in front of the television, long after I was supposed to be in bed, I found I was being addressed by a soft-spoken man, of sandy and thinning hair, and dressed in a washed-out rugby shirt. He was talking about something called The Pink Floyd and their new record, *Dark Side Of The Moon*. A mesmerising tune followed, accompanied by an animation of the outlines of three figures – synchronised dancers – flitting across the universe. It was terribly exotic. I was intrigued. Then, with further weekly forays into this secret late-night world, I was hooked.

In another programme, some musician I'd never heard of was being interviewed. Both guest and presenter were smoking and had bottles of beer open in front of them on the studio desk. Laid back was an inadequate description of *The Old Grey Whistle Test* back then.

Whistle Test gave me, and thousands of others, our first confirmed sightings of the wonders that were Neil Young & Crazy Horse, Little Feat, Randy Newman, Talking Heads, Rory Gallagher, John Martyn, Bob Marley & The Wailers, Joni Mitchell (I could go on for a couple of pages), all of whom would become my life-long companions. To be a viewer was to be a member of a private late-night club, open only to those of exquisitely good taste – most of the time. (Does anyone else recall the horrors of 'Stillwater, jamming'?) Back then, without the proliferation of television channels we have now, and without a huge range of music programmes, *Whistle Test* gave us the only opportunity we had to see groups we had read about in the music weeklies or heard – but not seen – on the John Peel programme. And they played *live* on the *OGWT*, unlike the showbiz mimers of *Top of the Pops*. With one's discovery of the *Test*, the latter became instantly a children's programme.

Little did I suspect that one day I would end up presenting the very same flagship programme that had been so formative in my adolescence, and had opened wide my musical tastes. (That was another happy accident, the full absurd story of which you can read in my autobiography, *No Off Switch*).

It was a bit of a shock, not just to find myself a presenter of the programme in the autumn of 1984, but to discover on my arrival just what a shoestring operation the *Whistle Test* was. In fact, the budget for the programme was so meagre, shoestrings would have been a luxury. We had no money for Autocue, the presenters' safety net. We wrote out the bones of our links in marker pen on huge sheets of white card. When I was doing a live introduction, Mark Ellen would stand next to the camera holding my prompt. When it was Mark's turn to speak to the nation, I would do the same for him. We became competitive: a particularly long and complicated link became known as 'a 3- Carder', which we felt daring to deliver and proud to do so without fluffing. Similarly, I can now reveal that the *Whistle Test's* trademark studio backgrounds – electrical ducting and air-conditioning pipes – were not the replica-utilitarian confection of some BBC design team; we simply couldn't afford to cover them up. Presenters' fees were equally basic.

Whistle Test was not mesmerised by fashion and celebrity and, in my era, not in the least deferential to rock stardom. Indeed, an appearance on the programme could be a sobering experience for many among rock's aristocracy. We were defiantly anti-fashion. We didn't give a bugger about whether we were regarded as hip or not. We were concerned with substance before style. We liked to trailblaze, to pioneer and, frequently, if we thought they were outstanding, to evangelise the unknown. *Whistle Test* – and here's the crucial difference – was journalism-driven.

I didn't care about the money, or the lack of it. During my three years as a presenter, 1984–1987, it was simply huge fun to work on the programme. Collaborating with presenters Mark Ellen and David Hepworth, *Whistle Test* was, for me, the music programme with A-Levels, made in the sixth-form common room (but only David had been made a prefect) under the direction of producer, Trevor Dann (who discovered me) and overseen – sort of – by the programme's editor and founder, Mike Appleton. Dear old Mike regarded us as a kindly but bewildered and bumbling headmaster in an Ealing comedy might have looked upon a school beyond his control. I am convinced that the *Whistle Test* of those years – three blokes having a whale of a time and sharing their enthusiasms irreverently with the nation – was the model for the *Top Gear* of two decades later.

The programme had, with my arrival, been given an overhaul by Trevor Dann. For many years it had been criticised for not keeping up with the times and for being too fixated with all that was soft and gentle and from the West Coast. This has some validity. For example, *Whistle Test's* strategy to deal with the upheaval of punk was to try to ignore it and hope it would go away so that we could all get back to listening to our Allman Brothers albums. But, fashionable though it became to mock the *OGWT*, it was also lazy to disregard how ground-breaking it had been and how absolutely right for its time it was for much of its life. And, for that earlier period, the languid apostle in the shape of Whispering Bob was its perfect presenter.

Bob was actually its second presenter, joining *OGWT* for the start of its second series in March 1972. Its original presenter, Richard Williams, had been the first choice of editor, Mike Appleton. The programme was Mike's baby, a spin-off from *Late Night Line-Up* on which Mike worked as a young producer. That first series, in 1971, was presented from the tiny studio normally occupied by the weatherman and – seriously – not much bigger than a cupboard.

The end came in 1987 when, in an internal BBC Television Centre reshuffle, *Whistle Test* was moved into the new, faddish department of Youth Programmes. We had never defined nor identified our audience by age, but by whether they liked good music or not. It was decided, however, that *Whistle Test* was not sufficiently 'cutting edge' – whatever that meant – and so the show's run was brought to an end, replaced by the now long-forgotten *Def II*. (Instantly forgettable at the time, come to think of it.) *Whistle Test's* execution was a kick in the teeth for thousands of loyal viewers.

But the *Whistle Test* refuses to die! At least in the memories and affections of the nation, so it seems. I am constantly asked still when, or whether, it will ever be brought back. I always reply that it has – long ago, in fact, disguised as *Later... with Jools Holland*. But there is one significant difference: can you imagine the national outcry if, in my *Whistle Test* days, I had insisted on banging along on, perhaps, a tambourine, in a cheeky-chappie fashion, with all the programmes' performing live guests?

Oh, and in case you were wondering: my favourite moment from among so many in my three lucky years as a *Whistle Test* presenter? I reckon the night we had the Ramones on live, and their opening number, at the top of the show, sending a posse of BBC safety officers scattering from the studio, towards the tea bar, in despair, still clutching their impotent noise meters.

Andy Kershaw

SIDE A

ALIASES

What's my real name?

1. Alvin Stardust

2. Adam Ant

3. Bono

4. Alice Cooper

5. Billy Idol

6. Elton John

7. Meat Loaf

8. Joni Mitchell

9. Iggy Pop

10. Lou Reed

11. Dusty Springfield

12. Sly Stone

13. Joe Strummer

14. Tina Turner

15. Barry White

ALL ABOUT THE USA

You (probably) know the song. But who's the artist?

1. 'Working For The Yankee Dollar'

2. 'Empire State Human'

3. 'Young Americans'

4. 'I'm So Bored With The USA'

5. 'Living In America'

6. 'Kids In America'

7. 'Volunteers'

8. 'All American Alien Boy'

9. 'American Pie'

10. 'American Woman' (original artist, 1970)

11. 'Breakfast In America'

12. 'I Hate America'

13. 'L'America'

14. 'Yankee Rose'

15. 'Surfin' USA'

ANIMALS

Who's the artist?

1. 'Pigs On The Wing'

2. 'Ben'

3. 'Rocky Raccoon'

4. 'Cheetah'

5. 'Save The Whales!'

6. 'I Love My Dog'

7. 'A Horse With No Name'

8. 'Salamanda Palaganda'

9. 'Penguin in Bondage'

10. 'Terrapin Station'

11. 'Seamus'

12. 'Crawling King Snake'

13. 'Coyote'

14. 'White Rabbit'

15. 'Rats And Monkeys'

BANNED RECORDS

1. Before his 1969 chart-topping version with Jane Birkin, Serge Gainsbourg recorded a version of 'Je T'Aime… Moi Non Plus' with which French actress?

2. The 1984 track 'Animal (Fuck Like A Beast)' was an early target for the PMRC, whose concern probably had something to do with the track being left off which band's self-titled debut?

3. What was Rolling Stone Mick Jagger forced to sing when the band performed 'Let's Spend The Night Together' on *The Ed Sullivan Show* in 1967?

4. Max Romeo's suggestive and ban-worthy 'Wet Dream' was an early reggae hit – but in which year?

5. Hawkwind were subject to a BBC ban for which 1973 single?

6. Which Beatles record cover depicted the band dressed in butcher smocks and holding raw meat and decapitated dolls?

7. Which 1970 hit got out of trouble by self-censoring its original mention of Coca-Cola?

8. One of punk's finest moments, issued to coincide with the Queen's Silver Jubilee in 1977, earned a chart blackout in a bid not to offend royalist sensibilities. What was the song?

9. Oddly not banned by the BBC, despite its references to transvesticism and a mid-song blow job, was which Lou Reed single from 1973?

10. Which Dead Kennedys single was banned in 1981, both by the BBC and many retailers, who weren't too impressed by the inclusion of the word 'fuck' in its title?

11. The *Two Virgins* album depicted John and Yoko naked on the cover, prompting a hasty cover up with most shops wrapping it in a plain brown wrapper. But what was the year that the sight of a Beatle penis caused a rumpus?

12. A reference to Ronald Reagan on a cult 1981 hit by Heaven 17 gave some radio stations the jitters. What was the explicitly titled record?

13. It was only an album track, but NWA's 'Fuck Tha Police' still came under a great deal of scrutiny when released in 1988. From which classic hip hop album did it come?

14. The implied innuendo in whose 1971 hit 'Brand New Key' secured it a partial radio ban in the States?

15. Under what recording name did Peter Cook and Dudley Moore release a series of comic and expletive-filled dialogues?

BEATLES COVERS

1. The pre-glam Ambrose Slade covered which song from the 'White Album'?

2. Phil Manzanera and Eno's mid-1970s progressive sideline 801 released a version of which pioneering Beatles album track?

3. The Damned stuck a version of which Beatles single on the flip of 'New Rose'?

4. Elvis Costello invoked which Fab anthem for his appearance at Live Aid?

5. The Carpenters revamped which Beatles single as a ballad?

6. Which singer gave Lennon and McCartney their first US hit when he took 'From Me To You' into the charts in 1963?

7. Which Woodstock performer capitalised on his success there by issuing a version of 'Here Comes The Sun' on single in 1971?

8. Björk's 1977 debut album featured the 11-year-old singing which Beatles song?

9. Judy Collins titled her 1966 album after which mid-1960s Beatles album track?

10. 'Ever So Lonely' hitmakers Monsoon turned to which Beatles song for the 1982 follow-up?

11. Aerosmith turned to which late-era Beatles song

for a single in 1978?

12. Which Motown artist revisited 'We Can Work It Out' on single in 1971?

13. Which 'Mad Dog' got in quick with a 1969 version of 'She Came In Through The Bathroom Window'?

14. Ray Charles turned to which mid-1960s Beatles hit for a 1967 single?

15. Taking a break from *Star Trek* in 1968, Captain James Kirk reverted back to being plain old William Shatner, though his version of a certain *Sgt Pepper* song was anything but humdrum.

CHARITY RECORDS

1. Jimmy Page, Eric Clapton, Jeff Beck and Steve Winwood were just some of the British rock legends who turned out for the ARMS concert at the Albert Hall in 1983. The event was the brainchild of which multiple sclerosis sufferer?

2. 1979 saw the first music-backed Secret Policeman's Ball, featuring Pete Townshend and Tom Robinson, and benefited which human rights organisation?

3. Who, at Live Aid in 1985, broke with the day's theme and mentioned the plight of the US farmers?

4. George Harrison's 1971 single, 'Bangla Desh', was released in response to the region's war and weather-prompted crisis. But which musician friend of the ex-Beatle sparked the idea?

5. In September 1972, Jesse Jackson introduced a host of black music legends at a series of concerts held over five days in Chicago, that were later worked into a documentary film. What was it called?

6. In 1985, Dionne Warwick and friends, including Stevie Wonder and Elton John, released which song as a fundraiser to benefit AIDS research?

7. 'God Save Us' was a 1971 fundraiser in support of the *Oz* magazine defendants facing an

obscenity court case. Which rock superstar was behind the record?

8. Who was the co-producer and Musical Director of the 'We Are The World' project?

9. The first in a series of Farm Aid concerts was organised for September 1985 by Neil Young and John Mellencamp in association with which US country music legend?

10. Which short series of US concerts in aid of Amnesty International in June 1986 ended with an all-star ensemble version of Bob Dylan's 'I Shall Be Released'?

11. Which major star almost didn't play at the Nelson Mandela 70th birthday Concert at Wembley because a vital piece of musical equipment went missing?

12. In October 1986, the first of a long-running series of fund-raising Bridge School Benefit concerts took place in California thanks to which musician and his wife?

13. Which pop and rock impresario was behind the 1979 Music For UNICEF concert that took place at the United Nations HQ in New York and starred the Bee Gees and ABBA?

14. Which progressive rock band released an album titled *Benefit* in 1971?

15. After its release, George Michael pledged the royalties for which 1984 Wham! single to benefit the Ethiopian famine appeal?

CHRISTMAS CRACKERS

Who got festive...

1. In 1977 with Bing Crosby?

2. In 1984 with 'Last Christmas'?

3. In 1985 with 'Merry Christmas Everyone'?

4. In 1981 with 'Christmas Wrapping'?

5. In 1973 (for the first of many times) with 'Merry Xmas Everybody'?

6. In 1976 with 'Ring Out, Solstice Bells'?

7. In 1980 with 'December Will Be Magic Again'?

8. In 1979 with 'Wonderful Christmastime'?

9. In 1987 (for the first time) with Kirsty MacColl?

10. In 1975 with 'In Dulci Jubilo'?

11. In 1972 with 'Happy Xmas (War Is Over)'?

12. In 1973 with 'Gaudete'?

13. In 1974 with 'Lonely This Christmas'?

14. In 1987 with 'Christmas In Hollis'?

15. In 1978 with 'Silent Night'?

CLASSIC ALBUM COVERS

The 1970s was the heyday for cover art. We're looking for the designer, unless specified…

1. *Osibisa* – Osibisa

2. *In Search Of Space* – Hawkwind

3. *Exile On Main St.* – Rolling Stones (photographer)

4. *Teaser And The Firecat* – Cat Stevens (artist)

5. *Cut* – The Slits (photographer)

6. *London Calling* – The Clash

7. *The Hissing Of Summer Lawns* – Joni Mitchell (artist)

8. *Diamond Dogs* – David Bowie

9. *Raw Power* – Iggy & the Stooges (photographer)

10. *American Beauty* – Grateful Dead

11. *Wish You Were Here* – Pink Floyd

12. *Ramones* – Ramones (photographer)

13. *Sticky Fingers* – Rolling Stones

14. *Country Life* – Roxy Music (concept)

15. *Tales From Topographic Oceans* – Yes

CLASSIC DEBUTS

But from which year?

1. *Horses* – Patti Smith

2. *All Things Must Pass* – George Harrison

3. *The Clash* – The Clash

4. *Led Zeppelin* – Led Zeppelin

5. *Gris Gris* – Dr John

6. *The B-52's* – The B-52's

7. *Appetite For Destruction* – Guns N' Roses

8. *The Kick Inside* – Kate Bush

9. *Can't Buy A Thrill* – Steely Dan

10. *Yo! Bum Rush The Show* – Public Enemy

11. *The Smiths* – The Smiths

12. *Black Sabbath* – Black Sabbath

13. *Unknown Pleasures* – Joy Division

14. *Funkadelic* – Funkadelic

15. *Blondie* – Blondie

CLASSIC LIVE ALBUMS

Argue amongst yourselves.
Then work out who the artists are.

1. *Kick Out The Jams*

2. *Live At Leeds* (released 1970)

3. *Space Ritual*

4. *Bless Its Pointed Little Head*

5. *Live-Evil*

6. *Live Dead*

7. *On Stage* (released 1970)

8. *Live: Meadowbrook, Rochester, Michigan 12th September 1971*

9. *Leftover Wine*

10. *Between Nothingness And Eternity*

11. *The Roxy London WC2 (Jan–Apr 77)*

12. *Performance: Rockin' The Fillmore*

13. *Roxy & Elsewhere*

14. *Dream Letter*

15. *Get Yer Ya-Ya's Out!*

CLASSICAL GAS

1. ELP drew on the work of which composer for 1971's *Pictures At An Exhibition*?

2. Which Tchaikovsky ballet was invoked by Keith Levine's guitar part on PiL's 1979 single, 'Death Disco'?

3. The Who turned which extract from Grieg's *Peer Gynt* into a 1967 album outtake freakout?

4. Which Malcolm McLaren album fused opera with contemporary music styles?

5. Deodato had a transatlantic hit in 1972 with a jazzed-up take on the theme from 2001, and originally which piece by Richard Strauss?

6. 1978's *An American Prayer*, featuring the Doors playing new music to old Jim Morrison poetry, drew on whose 'Adagio In G Minor' for the closing passages?

7. Which rock power trio struck lucky with 'Sabre Dance', based on a piece by the Russian composer Khachaturian?

8. Which composer gave his name to a showpiece for violinist Darryl Way on Curved Air's 1970 debut album, *Air Conditioning*?

9. Which classical piece welcomed the Rolling Stones on stage during their 1975 and 1976 tours?

10. The distinguished conductor Malcolm Arnold oversaw the Royal Philharmonic Orchestra's collaboration with which rock band for a 1969 live recording of *Concerto For Group And Orchestra*?

11. The Portsmouth Sinfonia played wonky versions of the classics with a little help from 1970s rock's most famous so-called 'non-musician'. Who was he?

12. ELO's breakthrough 45 was titled on classical lines. What was it?

13. During 'The Invocation & Ritual Dance Of The Young Pumpkin' on the *Absolutely Free* album, Frank Zappa's Mothers Of Invention played several repeated bars from which popular orchestral suite?

14. Which early Jethro Tull instrumental was based on a Bach lute piece?

15. Manfred Mann's Earthband's 1973 hit 'Joybringer' was based on which of Holst's *Planets*?

COLLABORATIONS

1.   A version of Johnny Kidd & The Pirates'
     'Please Don't Touch' was the lead cut on a
     1981 collaboration between Motörhead and
     Girlschool. What was the title of the EP?

2.   In 1973, Brian Eno released an album of
     experimental music with King Crimson guitarist
     Robert Fripp. What was it called?

3.   Maddy Prior and June Tabor joined forces in
     1976 with what self-deprecatingly titled album?

4.   What was the title of the 1977 Pete Townshend-
     Ronnie Lane collaboration?

5.   Isaac Hayes collaborated with which soul singer
     on the 1977 live double album, *A Man And A
     Woman*?

6.   'R.A.F.' was a one-off collaboration between
     Brian Eno and which New York punk vocal duo?

7.   *Birth Of Success* was a posthumous Jimi
     Hendrix album featuring pre-fame recordings
     made with which US R&B frontman?

8.   John Lydon teamed up with Time Zone, led by
     which hip hop originator, for the 1984 single
     'World Destruction'?

9.   What was the long-playing result of Carlos
     Santana's brief association with Alice Coltrane in
     1974?

10. Which band backed Donovan on his 1969 single, 'Goo Goo Barabajagal (Love Is Hot)'?

11. Who shared lead vocals with Diana Ross on the early 1969 Supremes / Temptations hit 'I'm Gonna Make You Love Me'?

12. Who was co-writer with Ringo Starr on the ex-Beatles' 1973 hit 'Photograph'?

13. Which New York 'No Wave' singer co-wrote and sang on Sonic Youth's 1985 'Death Valley '69' single?

14. Rick James collaborated with which leading Hollywood actor on the US Top 10 single, 'Party All The Time'?

15. Which vocal group helped on several songs on the Fun Boy Three's 1982 debut album?

COLOURS

1. 'Red Sails' appeared on which David Bowie album?

2. Which noted session musician came to prominence in 1968 as part of a club-style combo fronted by Andy Fairweather-Low?

3. The Stranglers' 'Golden Brown' was a Top 3 hit in which year?

4. 'Everything's Gone Green' for which indie dance act?

5. Who was the sometime Plastic Ono Band session man and drummer on Lennon's *Imagine* album?

6. Linda Ronstadt reworked whose old hit, 'Blue Bayou', in 1977?

7. While Paul Mauriat took the song to Number 1 in the USA in spring 1968, which noted guitarist had a crack at the Easy Listening instrumental 'Love Is Blue'?

8. Joni Mitchell's 'Big Yellow Taxi' was a hit in her native Canada in which year?

9. Les Gray was frontman with which glam rock combo?

10. Elvis Costello's early hit '(The Angels Wanna Wear My) Red Shoes' also appeared on which album?

11. Santana appended an instrumental to the version of 'Black Magic Woman' that appeared on their *Abraxas* album. What was it called?

12. Billy Idol's 'White Wedding' didn't become a hit in Britain until 1985. But when was it originally released?

13. What is Cilla Black's real name?

14. What was the colour of the snow Frank Zappa advised against eating?

15. Which blues musician inspired the 'Pink' half of the name Pink Floyd?

CONCEPT ALBUMS

1. Who cooked up the musical version of *War Of The Worlds*?

2. The Kinks released a series of concept albums in the 1970s. Which one included the minor chart hit, 'Sitting In The Midday Sun'?

3. What was the name of Serge Gainsbourg's 1971 concept album – with partner Jane Birkin playing both muse and title role?

4. Which classic four-sided concept record from 1973 was split into four themes – Truth, Knowledge, Culture and Freedom?

5. *Diamond Dogs* started life as David Bowie's attempt to bring which classic British novel to the stage?

6. Which 1974 concept album was subtitled *A Symphony By The Electric Light Orchestra*?

7. *The Butterfly Ball And The Grasshopper's Feast* was a 1974 concept album by which Deep Purple member?

8. Alice Cooper's first solo album was a journey through a child's dark imagination. What was it called?

9. Which one-time member of the Monkees released a 1974 concept project called *The Prison: A Book With A Soundtrack*?

10. Even punk acts weren't immune to the concept album idea, as Sham 69's second album confirmed. What was it called?

11. Who released the gritty solo concept project *White City: A Novel* in 1985?

12. Released late in 1968, *S.F. Sorrow* is sometimes hailed as the first concept album. Which band were responsible?

13. Having quit 10cc, Godley and Creme's first venture was to release a triple album exposition on the man versus nature conundrum. What was its title?

14. 1972's *Three Friends* was the first concept album for which British progressive rock group?

15. Yes's most ambitious work, *Tales From Topographic Oceans*, was based on ancient scriptural knowledge. Which band member left soon afterwards?

CONNECTIONS

What connects…

1. Creedence Clearwater Revival and Bill Wyman?

2. ELO and Wizzard?

3. Elvis Costello and Liv Tyler?

4. Donna Summer's 'I Feel Love' and the Rolling Stones' *Black And Blue*?

5. Echo And The Bunnymen and Jose Feliciano?

6. Hawkwind's *In Search Of Space* and The Damned's *Music For Pleasure*?

7. Marc Bolan and Marc Almond (aside from their first names)?

8. Which 1964 single by Marvin Gaye links The Band and the Small Faces?

9. Ian Gillan and Sweet drummer Mick Tucker?

10. Deep Purple and Siouxsie And The Banshees?

11. 'Heartbreak Hotel' and Three Dog Night's 'Joy To The World'?

12. Bon Jovi and Jimi Hendrix?

13. Joni Mitchell and Adam And The Ants?

14. The Damned and Curved Air?

15. Bob Dylan's *Nashville Skyline* and Leonard

Cohen's *Songs From A Room* – two 1969 albums produced by the same man. Who was he?

COVER VERSIONS

1. Whose 1984 debut album included cover versions of Gerry And The Pacemakers' 'Ferry Cross The Mersey' and Bruce Springsteen's 'Born To Run'?

2. One of David Bowie's lesser-known singles was 1980's wilfully abrasive cover of which Brecht and Weill cabaret tune?

3. Which singer in 1970 gave the Rolling Stones' 'Ruby Tuesday' an extraordinary makeover?

4. Which Beach Boys song did David Bowie cover on his 1984 *Tonight* album?

5. In what year did Sinead O'Connor's revamp of Prince's 'Nothing Compares 2 U' chart?

6. Who in 1976 had a hit with Springsteen's 'Blinded By The Light'?

7. 'Lady Marmalade' was initially a 1975 hit for which vocal group?

8. Who covered Tim Buckley's 'Song To The Siren' in 1983?

9. Which 1967 Dandy Livingstone song was revived in 1979 by the Specials?

10. The Monkees' 'I'm A Believer' was a hit in 1974 for which progressive rock luminary?

11. In what year did the Pet Shop Boys take Elvis

Presley's 'Always On My Mind' to Number 1 in Britain?

12. Who in 1974 first had the hit with 'I Will Always Love You'?

13. The Communards' 1986 chart-topper 'Don't Leave Me This Way' was originally a hit for who?

14. Whose 'Take Me To The River' was covered by Talking Heads in 1978?

15. Who gave Bread's 1972 hit 'Everything I Own' a reggae makeover in 1974?

A DATE WITH...

Fifteen classic pop 'n' rock moments – the month will do, but when did...

1. The Beatles play on the rooftop of the Apple HQ in Savile Row?

2. The Sex Pistols talk back to Bill Grundy on the *Today* show?

3. Bruce Springsteen make it to the cover of both *Time* and *Newsweek* magazines?

4. Roger Waters announce his departure from Pink Floyd?

5. The Woodstock Festival take place?

6. MTV launch?

7. Elvis Presley broadcast worldwide via satellite from Hawaii?

8. Grandmaster Flash's 'The Message' enter the British Top 30?

9. Paul McCartney announce that he'd quit The Beatles?

10. AC/DC's Bon Scott die after a night on the town?

11. Live Aid create history?

12. Pink Floyd start performing *The Dark Side Of The Moon* in concert?

13. The first compact disc go on sale (in Japan)?

14. Donna Summer's 'I Feel Love' enter the British singles chart?

15. Elvis Presley die?

DEAD FAMOUS

Fifteen Steps To Heaven

1.   Which original member of The Supremes was found dead in February 1976 aged 32?

2.   James Honeyman-Scott was one of two original members of The Pretenders who died during the early 1980s. Who was the other man?

3.   Which hard rock singer released two mid-1970s albums, *Teaser* and *Private Eyes*, before dying in 1976?

4.   Popular throughout the 1970s for her work with Fairport Convention, Fotheringay and as a soloist, Sandy Denny cut her teeth in 1967 as co-lead vocalist in which then little known folk-rock band?

5.   Which singer-songwriter had the misfortune of dying of a heroin overdose in the same month that John Lennon was shot?

6.   Who died when the private plane he was flying crashed in California in 1997?

7.   After three of Lynyrd Skynyrd were killed when their plane crashed in October 1977, two surviving members regrouped around which band name?

8.   Psychic TV scored a minor hit with 'Godstar', a 1986 tribute single dedicated to which late

1960s pop luminary?

9. Which high-profile Hollywood film director made his name with a short film based on the life of Karen Carpenter using Barbie dolls?

10. Stiv Bators was frontman with which Cleveland punk rockers?

11. Klaus Nomi was the first name musician to die of an AIDS-related illness in what year?

12. The singer of the Ruts was found dead in July 1980. Who was he?

13. Which member of Chicago shot himself?

14. The Grateful Dead's Pigpen died in 1973. What was his real name?

15. Who was the short-sighted, sweet-voiced and ecologically aware Canned Heat member who was found dead amidst his beloved redwood trees in 1970?

DISCO SUCKS

1.   Who was the Village People's producer/mentor?

2.   Which British synth-pop trio successfully revived Donna Summer's 1977 hit 'I Feel Love' in 1985?

3.   ABBA's least successful late 1970s hit was a rare, apocalyptic-sounding venture into disco. What was it?

4.   Yvonne Elliman, whose 'If I Can't Have You' was a huge *Saturday Night Fever* hit in 1978, spent much of the mid-1970s as backing singer for which British artist?

5.   Blondie's 1978 smash 'Heart Of Glass' was a new wave disco crossover classic. Who was the British producer who helped make it happen?

6.   KC And The Sunshine Band had two Number 1 US singles in 1975, 'Get Down Tonight' and a song that enjoyed a higher profile in Britain. What was it?

7.   Which Jacksons album included both 'Shake Your Body (Down To The Ground)' and 'Blame It On The Boogie'?

8.   What links Carl Douglas and Tina Charles?

9.   The Trammps' huge 1976 hit 'Disco Inferno' was preceded by a British Top 5 hit the previous year. What was it called?

10. Everyone knows about *Saturday Night Fever*, but what was the 1978 disco film that starred Jeff Goldblum and Debra Winger?

11. Which enormous disco legend was born Barry Eugene Carter?

12. Which 1977 disco hit later gave its title to a 1997 film starring Mark Wahlberg?

13. Which Chic song was written after Nile Rodgers and Bernard Edwards were refused entry to Studio 54?

14. Frank Zappa's satirical 'Disco Boy' appeared on his 1976 album *Zoot Allures*. But which Sheik Yerbouti number became an inadvertent disco favourite?

15. Who kicked off an extraordinary career by covering Tina Charles' 1976 hit 'I Love To Love' as an 11-year-old?

DON'T BE DAFT:
15 NOVELTY SONGS

But who was responsible for them?

1. 'Agadoo'

2. 'Bridget The Midget'

3. 'Mouldy Old Dough'

4. 'Eat It'

5. 'Disco Duck'

6. 'Orville's Song'

7. 'Gimme Dat Ding'

8. 'Shaddap You Face'

9. 'Loop Di Love'

10. 'The Chicken Song'

11. 'My Ding-A-Ling'

12. 'You're The One That I Want (comedy version)'

13. 'The Laughing Gnome'

14. 'The Birdie Song'

15. 'Kung Fu Fighting'

EARLIER BANDS / BAND NAMES

1. Todd Rundgren came of age on his 1973 *A Wizard, A True Star* album. But from which Yardbirds song did the name of his earlier, late 1960s band derive?

2. Who once were the Golliwogs?

3. Badfinger released one album for Apple under their original name the Iveys. What was it called?

4. Before he mutated into Simply Red, Mick Hucknall headed up which Manchester-based punk-era band?

5. How many records did the New Yardbirds release during the transition from the Yardbirds into Led Zeppelin?

6. The Sheffield-based Vice Versa mutated to become which 1980s pop smoothies?

7. Prior to their mid-1980s hard rock renaissance as The Cult, the Ian Astbury-fronted band were Goths known by an elongated version of that name. What was it?

8. Strontium 90 debuted at a day-long gig in Paris devoted to Gong and affiliated acts. Which huge new wave band did they become?

9. From punkish beginnings in Glasgow as Johnny

And The Self-Abusers, this band went on to become stadium rock stars during the 1980s and beyond. Who were they?

10. Who were Nick Cave's pre-Birthday Party group, whose debut album, *Door, Door*, was released while the band were still based in Melbourne, Australia?

11. A 1958 pre-Beatles acetate recording by the Quarrymen coupled an original, 'In Spite Of All The Danger', with a version of which Buddy Holly song?

12. The pre-fame Van Halen briefly went out as a) Genesis b) Van Gogh c) Van Der Graaf Generator?

13. Which duo first worked together in the 1950s as Tom and Jerry?

14. Who once were the Wailing Wailers?

15. Which ultra-hot late 1970s NYC-based dancefloor act had earlier gone out as the Big Apple Band?

EASY LISTENING: SLEEPING WITH THE ENEMY

1. Which German soundtrack specialist did Pulp sample for their 1998 single 'This Is Hardcore'?

2. What was the original title of Barry Manilow's 'Mandy'? a) 'Candy' b) 'Brandy' c) 'Randy'

3. Which bandleader and legendary MOR figure covered both Hawkwind's 'Silver Machine' and Alice Cooper's 'School's Out' in the early 1970s?

4. Amidst a string of huge successes during the 1970s was The Carpenters' 'A Kind Of Hush'. But which British pop act did it first?

5. After a prolific and successful 1960s, Burt Bacharach came a little unstuck with the soundtrack for a 1973 remake, starring Peter Finch and Sally Kellerman. What was it?

6. In 1976, the squeaky clean reputation of Andy Williams took a knock when his estranged wife, herself a singer, endured more than a spot of bother involving her ski instructor lover. Who was she?

7. Which record label was set up by Herb Alpert in the 1960s – ostensibly as a home for MOR music but later signing acts such as Humble Pie and The Police?

8. Which one-time prog rocker reinvented himself as the kaftan-wearing, falsetto voiced Forever And Ever man?

9. Which ska revival act revamped Andy Williams' hit 'Can't Get Used To Losing You' in 1983?

10. Who, in 1970, was the original Mood Indigo man – much sampled since the 1990s?

11. Throbbing Gristle pastiched the stylistic sensibility of the King of Exotica on the cover of their 1981 *Entertainment Through Pain* 'hits' collection. Who was he?

12. The Carpenters surprised everyone by throwing a massive guitar break into which 1972 hit?

13. Which vocal group had the blissed-out, Summer of Love hit in Britain with 'Up, Up And Away'?

14. Which one-time Amboy Dukes guitarist once announced that he wanted to buy the Muzak Corporation so that he could close it down?

15. Which gifted songwriting team wrote 'Anyone Who Had A Heart'?

EIGHTIES POP

1. Frankie Goes To Hollywood enjoyed an unprecedented run of three Number 1 UK hit singles with their first three releases. What was the title of the third?

2. In which year did the long-running various artist compilation album series *Now That's What I Call Music* begin?

3. Producer Tony Visconti's magic had worked with Marc Bolan, and with David Bowie, but he failed to revive Adam Ant's career in 1985 with which album?

4. Heidi Stern had a huge hit in 1985 with 'The Power Of Love'. What was her stage name?

5. Aztec Camera's second album, *Knife*, was produced by which AOR guitar legend?

6. After the collapse of Culture Club, Boy George resurrected his career with a 1987 solo Number 1 cover of which MOR band's 'Everything I Own'?

7. Kirsty MacColl had a Top 10 hit in the mid-1980s with whose song 'A New England'?

8. Before breaking out to form Yazoo, and later Erasure, Vince Clarke stayed long enough to record one album with Depeche Mode. Which one was it?

9. Who was the singer and songwriter behind the success of Talk Talk?

10. Who was Duran Duran's original bass-playing singer?

11. Yello came from a) Switzerland b) Swaziland c) Japan

12. Which synthpop soloist's 1982 debut album was titled *The Golden Age Of Wireless*?

13. What was the subtitle of the Pet Shop Boys' 1985 single 'Opportunities'?

14. Who was the moustachioed keyboard player in Soft Cell?

15. Which Orchestral Manoeuvres In The Dark album included the hits 'Souvenir', 'Joan Of Arc' and 'Maid Of Orleans'?

EPICS

1. What was the 23-minute epic that appeared on Genesis's 1972 album *Foxtrot*?

2. 'Karn Evil 9' took up half an hour of which Emerson, Lake & Palmer album?

3. 'The Low Spark Of High Heeled Boys' was a 12-minute title track for which rock-era legends?

4. Isaac Hayes's second album, released in 1969, included a version of Jimmy Webb's 'By The Time I Get To Phoenix' that clocked in at close to 20 minutes. What was its title?

5. The side-long, 10-part ultra-prog epic 'A Plague Of Lighthouse Keepers' was the crowning glory of which Van Der Graaf Generator record?

6. Which Led Zeppelin track was stretched to nearly 27 minutes on the 1976 soundtrack album *The Song Remains The Same*?

7. On which album did Pink Floyd's side-long epic 'Echoes' appear?

8. The title track to Rush's fourth studio album, released in 1976, took up the whole of side one. What was it called?

9. *Thick As A Brick* and *A Passion Play* – two Jethro Tull concept pieces. But which clocked in the longest?

10. The side-long 'Valentyne Suite' was the 1969 title track for which jazz-rock combo?

11. The live side of Mountain's *Flowers Of Evil* album was taken up by a Dream Sequence that began with a solo by the band's guitarist. Who was he?

12. Which Soft Machine album was made up of four side-long epics?

13. The first side of Donna Summer's 1975 second album was taken up with a smouldering title track. What was it?

14. The full-length version of Kraftwerk's 'Autobahn', as presented on their 1974 album, clocks in at close to a) 10 minutes b) 22 minutes c) 40 minutes

15. Which prolific frontman and songwriter wrote the 1971 hit 'Life's A Long Song'?

FAR-OUT ACID ROCK

Who's the artist?

1.   'White Rabbit'

2.   'Third Stone From The Sun'

3.   'Section 43'

4.   'Interstellar Overdrive'

5.   'Tales Of Brave Ulysses'

6.   'I Can See For Miles'

7.   'Dear Mr Fantasy'

8.   'Who Do You Love'

9.   'Tomorrow Never Knows'

10. 'Time Has Come Today'

11. 'Trust Us'

12. 'Ball And Chain'

13. 'We Love You'

14. 'The End'

15. 'Signed D.C. (Out Here version)'

FESTIVALS

1. Which band was scheduled to support The Who at their open-air Charlton gig in May 1974 but cancelled when their singer was badly beaten up in Staines?

2. The inspiration behind WOMAD, it was inevitable that Peter Gabriel would play at the first WOMAD festival, which took place at Shepton Mallet in Somerset. But in what year?

3. One-time television host and prankster Jeremy Beadle was partly responsible for organising which 1972 rock festival, with Captain Beefheart and the Grateful Dead among the main acts?

4. Which year's Reading Festival, which saw bottles of urine hurled towards Bonnie Tyler and similar unsavoury endeavours, prompted a rethink of the annual event?

5. Kim Weston, the Staple Singers and Isaac Hayes were among the performers at which 1972 event sometimes regarded as the African-American Woodstock?

6. There were no tents or green spaces at the 100 Club Punk Rock Festival in September 1976, but there was – perhaps predictably – a nasty incident that led to the arrest of which Sex Pistols superfan?

7. Which annual Cornish music festival, which ran

between 1981 and 1986, included Siouxsie And The Banshees, The Fall and The Cure among its headliners?

8.   The Grateful Dead, The Band and the Allman Brothers headlined which 600,000-strong US rock festival in July 1973?

9.   Queen, AC/DC and Rod Stewart headlined the first Rock In Rio Festival in which year?

10. Jefferson Airplane, Tyrannosaurus Rex and the Crazy World Of Arthur Brown played the Isle Of Wight Festival in a) 1968 b) 1969 c) 1970?

11. Which rock subculture entrepreneur sold Teddy Boy accoutrements to the crowds at the London Rock And Roll Show in 1972?

12. Which band headlined the 1979 Knebworth Festival?

13. David Bowie, Melanie, Traffic and Arthur Brown's Kingdom Come were just some of the underground acts who made it to the first Glastonbury Fayre proper in which year?

14. John Lennon and Alice Cooper lined up alongside numerous 1950s rockin' legends at which 1969 festival in Canada?

15. Rainbow and Scorpions topped the bill at the first Donington Festival. But what was the year?

FIFTH BEATLE

Which Fifth Beatle claimant...

1. Played keyboards on 'Get Back'?

2. Drove the van then ran the Apple empire?

3. Was the band's bass player in 1960 and the early months of 1961?

4. Produced almost all of their records?

5. Led a 1970s band noted for their Beatles-like string section?

6. Managed the group during their key years?

7. Was the drummer that Ringo Starr officially replaced?

8. Learned his DJ trade in the States during the early and mid-1960s by virtue of sharing the same Liverpudlian accent as The Beatles?

9. Was the guitarist that made a distinctive, though uncredited, contribution to a George Harrison song on the 'White Album'?

10. Was the only Beatle wife who attended practically every recording session during the band's final years?

11. Was the group's road manager who was later killed in a police shoot-out?

12. Ran Indica Books and introduced the band to

key underground texts and figures during the mid-1960s?

13. Was brought in by Lennon, Harrison and Starr early in 1969 to rescue the ailing Apple organisation?

14. Set up Northern Songs in 1962 to publish Lennon and McCartney's songwriting?

15. Was the band's influential PR man and bon vivant at Apple Records HQ?

FILM CONNECTION / SCREEN DREAMS

1. The original idea for a Sex Pistols film was 'Who Killed Bambi?' directed by which specialist in ample-bosomed cinematography?

2. Which actor released a bizarre personality album where his TV sleuth Jason King alter ego was invoked for several songs?

3. Donna Summer had a hit with it in 1978, but which British actor took 'MacArthur Park' into the charts a decade earlier?

4. J. Geils Band singer Peter Wolf was once married to which Hollywood actress?

5. Crispian Mills, who went on to front 1990s band Kula Shaker, is the son of which distinguished British actress?

6. Joe Strummer appeared in which 1987 Alex Cox film?

7. The 1993 Tina Turner biopic was titled after which hit single released nine years earlier?

8. Ray Davies wrote, directed and scored his own film project in 1984. What was it called?

9. Which song did the Psychedelic Furs re-record for the soundtrack of a 1986 film that shared the same title?

10. Before it was dusted off for royalty, 'Candle In The Wind' was Elton John's sympathetic take on the life of which Hollywood actress?

11. The moody shot of US actor Joe Dallesandro on the cover of The Smiths' debut album comes from which film?

12. Which member of Spandau Ballet ended up in the long-running British soap opera *EastEnders*?

13. Which Hollywood actor is the brother of the man who wrote 'Wild Thing' and the father of Angelina Jolie?

14. Which gospel legend sings 'Trouble Of The World' at the climax of the 1959 weepie *Imitation Of Life*?

15. Simple Minds' huge 1985 success with 'Don't You (Forget About Me)' was partly down to the song's appearance in which film?

FILMS IN SONG

1. Kim Carnes sang about which vintage film star in her 1981 hit?

2. Which US singer-songwriter newcomer had Marlene on her wall in 1985?

3. Adam And The Ants reckoned which British actor wore 'White Sox' in 1979?

4. Roxy Music's '2HB' was a cryptic homage to which Hollywood icon?

5. Who reckoned 'John Wayne Is Big Leggy'?

6. Robert De Niro was waiting in 1984 – but for who?

7. Whose 'The Ballad Of Dwight Fry' celebrated a long-forgotten actor famous for his supporting roles in Hollywood horror films?

8. Who in 1973 sang about the 'Cracked Actor'?

9. Which US band revived the 1944 film title *Thirty Seconds Over Tokyo* for their 1975 debut single?

10. 1980s Scottish rockers Big Country evoked a 1958 Western film starring which Hollywood icon?

11. 400 Blows were an early 1980s post-punk band named after a 1959 film directed by which noted new wave film auteur?

12. Which James Cagney film later became a hit song for Sham 69?

13. Which San Franciscan experimentalists named a 1982 12" after a Greta Garbo satirical comedy, *Ninotchka*?

14. Which song on David Bowie's 1976 *Station To Station* album was originally recorded by Johnny Mathis for a 1957 film soundtrack?

15. Which Scott Walker song was directly inspired by a 1957 Ingmar Bergman film classic?

GLAM

1. Who was California's instant flop glam rock idol?

2. The pre-fame Bay City Rollers were briefly known by what name?

3. Rob Davis is one of 21st-century pop's leading songwriters, with Kylie Minogue's 'Can't Get You Out Of My Head' among his many hits. But back in the days of glam rock, he was the effete, earring-wearing guitarist with which revivalist combo?

4. Chicory Tip's 'Son Of My Father' was such a huge Number 1 hit in 1972 that it has tended to obscure their two subsequent Top 20 hits. Name either of them.

5. Wizzard brought some big-band oomph to glam rock. But in 1973, frontman Roy Wood had a hit with which unusual ballad?

6. What was the theme song for Slade's surprisingly gritty 1975 feature film?

7. Prior to his emergence as a photogenic pop star, David Essex had been the star of which stage musical?

8. Which songwriting team masterminded numerous hits for Sweet, Mud and Suzi Quatro?

9. In which US city did Suzi Quatro pay her dues

before her arrival in London?

10. Who was the musical brains behind Gary Glitter?

11. Which Sweet hit began with the words, 'Are you ready, Steve?'

12. Which bunch of glammed-up rockers boasted guitarist Ariel Bender in their ranks?

13. What was the Glitter Band's first Top 10 hit?

14. Which of Sparks's Mael brothers played keyboards and sported a Hitlerian 'tache?

15. A mainstream 1960s singer gave David Bowie's career a boost in 1971 by scoring a Top 20 hit with 'Oh! You Pretty Things'. Who was he?

GLAM RACKET

Shiny, anthemic, memorable... Who was the artist?

1. 'Solid Gold Easy Action'

2. 'All The Young Dudes'

3. 'Ball Park Incident'

4. 'Baby's On Fire'

5. 'Teenage Rampage'

6. 'Drive-In Saturday'

7. 'Jet Boy'

8. 'Always Yours'

9. 'Rock On'

10. 'Can The Can'

11. 'Stay With Me'

12. 'Cum On Feel The Noize'

13. 'School's Out'

14. 'This Town Ain't Big Enough For Both Of Us'

15. 'Virginia Plain'

GOING IT ALONE

Sometimes it's to freshen up, though occasionally it leads to an entirely new career. Which well-established band members decided to go it alone with the following (not necessarily debut) albums...

1. *Fish Rising*

2. *Thanks I'll Eat It Here*

3. *She's The Boss*

4. *Everything Is Everything*

5. *Arc Of A Diver*

6. *Rich Man's Woman*

7. *Roots*

8. *Deep In the Heart Of Nowhere*

9. *White Snake*

10. *Got To Be There*

11. *Annie In Wonderland*

12. *Songs For A Tailor*

13. *World Shut Your Mouth*

14. *Exposure*

15. *My Whole World Ended*

GREAT LABELS

Great albums all – but we're after the classic labels...

1. *McLemore Avenue* – Booker T. & The MGs

2. *Psychocandy* – The Jesus And Mary Chain

3. *A Wizard, A True Star* – Todd Rundgren

4. *I Want To See The Bright Lights Tonight* –
    Richard and Linda Thompson

5. *Bigger & Deffer* – LL Cool J

6. *Electric Ladyland* – Jimi Hendrix Experience

7. *Meat Is Murder* – The Smiths

8. *Welcome To The Pleasure Dome* – Frankie Goes
    To Hollywood

9. *Reflections* – The Supremes

10. *Greetings From LA* – Tim Buckley

11. *Songs About Fucking* – Big Black

12. *African Herbsman* – Bob Marley & The Wailers

13. *One Step Beyond* – Madness

14. *Prayers On Fire* – The Birthday Party

15. *Damaged* – Black Flag

GUESTS

1. Who was the violin player on Bob Dylan's mid-1970s *Rolling Thunder Revue*?

2. Which Beatle made an uncredited appearance on the Beach Boys' *Smiley Smile* album track 'Vegetables'?

3. Keith Richards' first guest appearance with Tom Waits came on which album?

4. Which Miles Davis album featured a cameo by Sting impersonating a French policeman?

5. Which one-time Hammond organist with Arthur Brown and Atomic Rooster guested on Dexy's Midnight Runners' 1985 album *Don't Stand Me Down*?

6. Humble Pie drummer Jerry Shirley also backed which late 1960s psychedelic renegade on record and in concert?

7. Who played lead guitar on David Bowie's 1970 single 'The Prettiest Star'?

8. Carly Simon's 1972 hit 'You're So Vain' featured whose unmistakable voice behind her?

9. Which virtuoso keyboard player sat in on the session for T. Rex's 'Get It On'?

10. Who contributed a harmonica solo to Eurythmics' 'There Must Be An Angel (Playing With My Heart)'?

11. One of Whitney Houston's first lead vocals was recorded with which group of New York-based rock experimentalists?

12. Which prog band drummer joined fellow rock luminaries John Cale and Robert Fripp for Eno's third solo set, *Another Green World*?

13. Whose 1980 solo album, his third, featured cameos from Kate Bush and Paul Weller?

14. She sang backing vocals with the Slits and New Age Steppers, and stepped up front with Rip Rig + Panic and Float Up CP. Who was she?

15. Who was the drummer on Jimi Hendrix's *Band Of Gypsys* album?

GUITARISTS

1. In autumn 1970, a guitarist named John Genzale Jr. joined an aspiring New York band then calling themselves Actress. Under which name was he better known?

2. John Denver sang about 'Rocky Mountain High'. But which guitarist was responsible for the 1973 US radio hit 'Rocky Mountain Way'?

3. Which British jazz-rock guitarist lent his name to a track released by Miles Davis?

4. Whose 'Bolero' also featured Keith Moon, Jimmy Page, John Paul Jones and Nicky Hopkins?

5. Eddie Van Halen arguably redefined the art of guitar playing with which instrumental track from the band's 1978 debut album?

6. Mark Knopfler formed Dire Straits with a younger brother. Who was he?

7. Brian May's keen interest in astronomy and space travel was reflected in the title of his first solo project, a 1983 mini-album credited to 'Brian May + Friends'. And it was...?

8. Who was the acid-funk guitar master on the first three Funkadelic albums?

9. Which producer controversially overdubbed new parts on Jimi Hendrix recordings for a series of three albums issued in the mid-1970s?

10. Who was guitarist in Henry Cow?

11. Yes guitarist Steve Howe started off with which psychedelic era underground act?

12. What was Robin Trower's 1974 breakthrough chart album?

13. Who was Booker T's legendary guitarist?

14. Eric Clapton changed gear in 1974 with *461 Ocean Boulevard*. In which US state could the location be found?

15. Roxy Music guitarist Phil Manzanera revived an earlier band in 1975 for a one-off album, *Mainstream*. Who were they?

HARD ROCK AND METAL

1. Who was the influential DJ and early Maiden supporter who came up with the *Metal For Muthas* compilation idea?

2. The producer was Todd Rundgren, the writers were Goffin and King and the song was 'The Loco-Motion'. But which hard rock band took it to the top of the US singles chart in 1974?

3. Which song did Whitesnake re-record, earning them a US Number 1 in 1987?

4. Who replaced the departing Dave Mustaine in Metallica?

5. Which San Francisco-based power trio charted in the USA in 1968 with a heavily distorted take on Eddie Cochran's 'Summertime Blues'?

6. What instrument does Mötley Crüe's Nikki Sixx play?

7. Which Cult album, released in 1987, marked the band's full transformation from Goth to hard rock?

8. What was the last Metallica album recorded with bassist Cliff Burton?

9. Dutch 1970s rock band Golden Earring were fronted by a man with a suspiciously British-sounding name. What was it?

10. Which band sang, on a 1968 single, of 'heavy metal thunder'?

11. Southern rockers Black Oak Arkansas were probably best known for their flamboyant frontman. Who was he?

12. Prior to 1987's *Appetite For Destruction* album, Guns N' Roses released a limited edition live EP. What was it called?

13. Aerosmith received a huge boost in 1986 when Run-DMC brought them on board for a rap-metal take on 'Walk This Way'. The song had first appeared in 1975 on which Aerosmith album?

14. Meat Loaf fronted *Bat Out Of Hell*, his massive 1978 rock epic, but who was his songwriting collaborator?

15. The phrase New Wave Of British Heavy Metal was associated with which British rock music weekly?

HARD-UP HEROES

1.   Which 1969 cut recorded by Python Lee Jackson with guest singer Rod Stewart was revived on single in 1972?

2.   Which future punk anti-hero released a 1976 single, 'Silly Billy', as Mari Elliott?

3.   Prior to his 1970 breakthrough, which future superstar recorded copycat versions of the hits of the day for a series of budget LP releases?

4.   Which guitarist backed Rosa Lee Brooks on a little-known 1965 single, 'My Diary'?

5.   And which future psychedelic cult legend wrote the song?

6.   Which subsequent stadium legends began life in the mid-1980s as On A Friday?

7.   Before forming the Rolling Stones, Mick Jagger, Keith Richards and future Pretty Thing Dick Taylor recorded themselves rehearsing at home, including a version of Richie Valens' 'La Bamba', as what aspiring R&B combo?

8.   Prior to joining Jefferson Airplane, Grace Slick had already been performing future hits 'Somebody To Love' and 'White Rabbit' with which aspiring acid-rock act?

9.   Who warmed up for her later success in 1960s all-women bands the Pleasure Seekers and Cradle?

10. Adam And The Ants released their first 45, 'Young Parisians', on which distinctly un-punkish label?

11. Which future rock legend did a short stint in 1959 backing bobbysoxer singer Bobby Vee?

12. The origins of which leading glam rock band can be found in mid-1960s combo the 'N Betweens?

13. Who between spring 1977 and spring 1978 were known as the Hype?

14. Prior to his mid-1970s success, which US frontman had a one-off US hit in 1968 with 'Ramblin' Gamblin' Man'?

15. Tony Visconti recorded a single as Dib Cochran & The Earwigs with which future superstar on guitar?

HE'S THE BOSS – AND SO IS SHE!

We're looking for the act each manager is most closely associated with.

1. Brian Epstein

2. Malcolm McLaren

3. Peter Grant

4. Rob Gretton

5. Bernie Rhodes

6. Sharon Osbourne

7. Tony Secunda

8. Andrew Loog Oldham

9. Tony Defries

10. Robert Stigwood

11. Rod Smallwood

12. Tony Smith

13. Herb Cohen

14. Steve O'Rourke

15. Chas Chandler

HIP HOP

1. Which hip hop spokesman famously described rap as 'black people's CNN'?

2. Who in 1989 were *3 Feet High And Rising*?

3. What was the title of LL Cool J's Rick Rubin-produced 1985 debut album?

4. *Rhyme Pays* was the 1987 debut for which future hip hop icon?

5. Rick Rubin founded Def Jam Recordings in 1984 with whom?

6. Public Enemy's DJ gets name-checked intermittently on 1987's 'Rebel Without A Pause'. Who is he?

7. Which early New York hip hop pioneer is also behind the Universal Zulu Nation?

8. Which MC was the main voice in Grandmaster Flash And The Furious Five?

9. Whose 1987 *Criminal Minded* album is credited with launching gangsta rap?

10. Years before it was remixed into a huge international hit single, 'It's Like That' appeared on Run-DMC's self-titled debut album in which year?

11. DJ Kool Herc is credited with kick-starting hip hop in which district of New York?

12. Who brought the words of Malcolm X into the British singles chart in 1983 with his 'No Sell Out' mash-up?

13. Who, in 1987, were 'Paid In Full'?

14. 'Walk This Way', a hit collaboration between Run-DMC and Aerosmith, was originally a hit for the rock group early in which year?

15. Slayer guitarist Kerry King guests on which early Beastie Boys classic?

HOBBIES

1. This shock rocker adores golf and films.

2. Once imprisoned on a drugs charge, this Rolling Stone is much happier these days with a good seat at Lords cricket ground.

3. Which Pink Floyd man has a passion for racing cars?

4. From the Small Faces to the Faces to The Who to... the polo field. Who is he?

5. This Guns N' Roses man is said to have a room full of pinball machines.

6. Which Motörhead man has revealed a penchant for Nazi memorabilia?

7. This blond Iron Maiden guitarist has a big golfing habit.

8. Another Maiden man is an airline pilot.

9. Which world-famous guitarist received his PhD in Astrophysics in 2007?

10. The third floor of whose Beverly Hills mansion is apparently filled with a huge model train set complete with numerous hand-built fittings?

11. Which stony-faced Stone collects artefacts from the American Civil War?

12. The Queen of Soul likes nothing better than to crochet.

13. Which guitarist's guitarist builds his own hot rods?

14. A founding father of hip hop apparently owns around 5,000 mugs.

15. Which ex-Runaway is now a chainsaw artist?

JAZZ ROCK

1. Which Mahavishnu Orchestra album was produced by George Martin?

2. Pete Townshend made light of a reference to jazz pianist Mose Allison as 'a jazz sage' on a reissue of which Who album?

3. Herbie Hancock embraced a funk-inspired jazz fusion sound in 1973 with which album?

4. Which soul-jazz guitarist came of age in the mid-1970s with the *Breezin'* album?

5. Jan Hammer, he of the 1985 hit with the *Miami Vice* theme, was once keyboard player in which early 1970s jazz-rock virtuoso band?

6. The ECM label emerged at the forefront of contemporary jazz during the 1970s. With which pianist is the label most closely associated?

7. 1972's *Caravanserai* marked a significant leap into jazz for which band?

8. Which bassist worked closely with Chick Corea in Return To Forever?

9. Who was Gong's distinctive flautist sax player?

10. Thanks largely to their jazz leanings, Soft Machine were the first rock band to play the Proms – but in which year?

11. Which jazz-literate rock musician famously

insisted that jazz wasn't dead, but that it 'just smells funny'.

12. *The Sound Of 65* was a pioneering beat-era album by a group led by which organist/singer?

13. What was the name of the blistering quartet led by drummer Tony Williams at the start of the 1970s?

14. A British-born bassist joined Miles Davis for his pioneering *In A Silent Way* and *Bitches Brew* albums. Who was he?

15. Which guitarist led the mid-1970s fusion band the Eleventh House?

KRAUTROCK

1. After 1970's *Yeti*, Amon Duul II released a second double-album the following year. What was it?

2. Which Krautrock legend earned a rare tribute from The Fall on their 1985 album *This Nation's Saving Grace*?

3. In 1995, ex-Teardrop Explodes frontman Julian Cope wrote and published a book on Krautrock. What was its title?

4. Which Krautrock band received a huge push in 1973 when new record label Virgin released a collection of outtakes for the price of a single?

5. *Electronic Meditation* from 1970 was the debut album for which subsequently more serene Krautrock band?

6. Several years after Krautrock's heyday, pop mavericks Trio just missed out on a UK Number 1 with which naggingly insistent single?

7. Which US hardcore trio recorded a version of Kraftwerk's 'The Model' for their 1987 album *Songs About Fucking*?

8. Can's first frontman was which African-American poet/singer?

9. Who is the Amon Duul II frontwoman whose voice sounds uncannily similar to that of PiL-era John Lydon, a teenage Krautrock enthusiast?

10. Which Faust album included an instrumental titled 'Krautrock'?

11. Ex-Kraftwerk renegades Klaus Dinger and Michael Rother formed which influential Krautrock duo in 1971?

12. Kraftwerk hailed from which German city?

13. Popol Vuh provided several soundtracks for which acclaimed German filmmaker?

14. Which legendary Krautrock producer/engineer started his career working for both Marlene Dietrich and Karlheinz Stockhausen?

15. Rebop Kwaku Baah and Rosko Gee joined Can in 1977 having both played with which top British rock combo?

LABEL ASSOCIATIONS

With which labels are the
following acts best associated?

1. Elvis Presley

2. The Temptations

3. Dusty Springfield

4. Beach Boys

5. Bob Marley

6. Patti Smith

7. Pink Floyd

8. The Doors

9. Talking Heads

10. The Specials

11. Chuck Berry

12. The Carpenters

13. Blondie

14. Kate Bush

15. Dr. Feelgood

LOVE MUSIC

Who sang these songs of love and... lust?

1. 'Love Song' (the punk song)

2. 'Radar Love'

3. 'Love Don't Live Here Anymore'

4. 'Chequered Love'

5. 'One Love' (the reggae song)

6. 'Love Train'

7. 'This Is Not A Love Song'

8. 'Can't Get Enough Of Your Love Babe'

9. 'Love Like A Man'

10. 'Love Cats'

11. 'The Meaning Of Love'

12. 'Big Love'

13. 'Love Shack'

14. 'Love Comes In Spurts'

15. 'Genius Of Love'

MATCH THE SINGER AND THE BAND

1.   Bryan Ferry

2.   Ian Anderson

3.   Eric Carmen

4.   Larry Blackmon

5.   Errol Brown

6.   David Thomas

7.   Phil Lynott

8.   Lionel Ritchie

9.   Edwyn Collins

10. Geddy Lee

11. Bret Michaels

12. Roger Hodgson

13. Pauline Black

14. Dave Vanian

15. David Byrne

MISSING WORDS: ALBUM TITLES

1. *Damn The* * (Tom Petty And The Heartbreakers)

2. *Songs In The Key Of* * (Stevie Wonder)

3. *The* * *On The Door* (The Cure)

4. *Fly Like An* * (Steve Miller Band)

5. *A New* * Record (ELO)

6. *Free Your Mind ... And Your* * *Will Follow* (Funkadelic)

7. *Street* * (Lou Reed)

8. * *Weeks* (Van Morrison)

9. *Another* * *In A Different Kitchen* (Buzzcocks)

10. *Best Dressed* * *In Town* (Dr. Alimantado)

11. *Knocked Out* * (Bob Dylan)

12. *Our Favourite* * (Style Council)

13. *Cupid And* * *85* (Scritti Politti)

14. *In The Wake Of* * (King Crimson)

15. * *Connection* (Parliament)

MISSING WORDS: BAND NAMES

1. Brinsley *

2. * Images

3. The * Explodes

4. The * Alex Harvey Band

5. Kevin Ayers And The * World

6. * Below Zero

7. Edgar Winter's White *

8. Link * And His Ray Men

9. * Beefheart And His Magic Band

10. * X

11. Ronnie Lane's Slim *

12. *, Hands & Feet

13. Back * Crawler

14. Joan Jett & The *

15. Eric * & Rakim

MISSING WORDS: SONG TITLES

1. Run To The * (Iron Maiden)

2. * Spirit (Brian Eno & David Byrne)

3. Like A * (Neil Young)

4. Nice 'n' * (Stranglers)

5. Love Comes In * (Richard Hell & The Voidoids)

6. My Old * (Diana Ross)

7. No Time To Be * (Adverts)

8. Don't * The Reaper (Blue Oyster Cult)

9. Summer * City (ABBA)

10. Back Street * (Curved Air)

11. Down The * (Status Quo)

12. * So Good (Susan Cadogan)

13. We Are The * (David Bowie)

14. Get The * Right (Depeche Mode)

15. Sweet * Alabama (Lynyrd Skynyd)

MONTHS

1. Which British pop act hit Number 1 in 1975 with a song called 'January'?

2. In what London concert hall did Pink Floyd's 1967 *Games For May* extravaganza take place?

3. Soft Machine's 'Moon In June' was a virtuoso piece for the band's singing drummer. Who was he?

4. Which late-1960s West London psychedelic act are best known for their song 'Dandelion Seeds'?

5. What was the title of Neil Diamond's iconic 1972 live album?

6. Which long-established vocal group hit a rich seam of British hit singles starting in 1978 with a song called 'September'?

7. What month in 1981 saw the release of U2's second album, *October*?

8. Who in 1987 had a Top 10 hit with 'April Skies'?

9. On which 1970 song did John Lennon advise us never to forget the fifth of November?

10. '4th Of July, Asbury Park (Sandy)' first appeared on which Bruce Springsteen album?

11. 'The Ides Of March' was a short instrumental opener on whose second album, *Killers*?

12. 'First Of May' was a 1969 Top 10 hit for which successful act?

13. 'Night Of The 4th Of May' appeared on which singer-songwriter's 1972 album, *Orange*?

14. 'August' was the opening song on Love's fourth album, released in 1969. What was the title?

15. 'September Song' has been covered by a range of artists including James Brown, Bryan Ferry and Echo & The Bunnymen's Ian McCullough. Who was the Berlin-based composer who wrote it?

NEW WAVE

1. The Stiff Tour of 1977 featured Elvis Costello, Ian Dury, Nick Lowe, Wreckless Eric and one long-haired renegade from Ladbroke Grove freak combo Pink Fairies. Who was he?

2. Which new wave band debuted in spring 1975 as Tiger Lily with a cover of Fats Waller's 'Ain't Misbehavin"?

3. Which new wave artist once recorded a song titled 'Bay City Rollers We Love You' in order to get out of a recording contact?

4. Everyone remembers The Boomtown Rats' huge 1979 hit 'I Don't Like Mondays', but which album did it come from?

5. The pre-Tom Robinson Band Cafe Society were talent-spotted by which 1960s rock and pop luminary?

6. After his self-referencing Top 5 single in 1978, Jilted John man Graham Fellows reinvented himself as which character, beloved of BBC Radio 4 listeners?

7. Two ex-members of The Strawbs, Richard Hudson and John Ford, adopted a 'punk' disguise for a handful of 45s at the end of the 1970s. What was it?

8. Prior to finding fame with Simply Red, Mick Hucknall was vocalist with which Manchester-

based late 1970s punk-pop quartet?

9. UB40's 1980 hit debut 45, 'King', was a tribute song dedicated to a) Billie-Jean King b) Elvis Presley c) Martin Luther King Jr

10. Who was The Jam's drummer?

11. A 1980 album *The Up Escalator* brought US success to which band?

12. In summer 1979, ex-Slik and Rich Kids frontman Midge Ure stepped in and toured with which band? a) The Pop Group b) Darts c) Thin Lizzy?

13. Who, according to the 1980 Undertones single, was a winner at Subbuteo?

14. Who, in 1980, asked, 'Do You Dream In Colour'?

15. Devo came from which Ohio city?

NEW WAVE, OLD WAVE

Who had the original hit with the following new wave-era singles?

1. 'Denis' (Blondie)

2. 'I Only Want To Be With You' (Tourists)

3. 'You've Lost That Lovin' Feelin'' (Human League)

4. 'I Second That Emotion' (Japan)

5. 'I Want Candy' (Bow Wow Wow)

6. 'Mony Mony' (Billy Idol)

7. 'You're A Better Man Than I' (Sham 69)

8. 'Take Me To The River' (Talking Heads)

9. 'I Think We're Alone Now' (Lene Lovich)

10. 'Money' (Flying Lizards)

11. 'Captain Of Your Ship' (Bette Bright And The Illuminations)

12. 'Running Away' (The Raincoats)

13. '(I Can't Get No) Satisfaction' (Devo)

14. 'Stop Your Sobbing' (Pretenders)

15. 'Nights In White Satin' (Dickies)

NUMBER 2s

But what was the year they stalled?

1. 'You Sexy Thing' – Hot Chocolate

2. 'All Right Now' – Free

3. 'Dance Away' – Roxy Music

4. 'Radio Gaga' – Queen

5. 'Temptation' – Heaven 17

6. 'Torch' – Soft Cell

7. 'Golden Brown' – Stranglers

8. 'Modern Love' – David Bowie

9. 'Pop Muzik' – M

10. 'Never Can Say Goodbye' – Gloria Gaynor

11. 'The Jean Genie' – David Bowie

12. 'Children Of The Revolution' – T. Rex

13. 'Young Hearts Run Free' – Candi Staton

14. 'Funkytown' – Lipps Inc

15. 'Manic Monday' – Bangles

NUMBERS

1. Who were 'Lookin' After No. 1'?

2. She duetted with Marvin Gaye for 'It Takes Two'.

3. Which heavy rock band bashed out 'Four Sticks'?

4. Who, all dressed up in space-age clobber, claimed that all we had left were 'Five Years'?

5. You can be guaranteed that *The Number Of The Beast* that this NWOBHM band had in mind was 666.

6. Whose wayward voice sang about a 'Lucky Number'?

7. Which band boasted that 'your number' was written on the back of their hand?

8. 'The Numberer' was the B-side to which Roxy Music hit?

9. Which early 1980s electronic duo managed to get a raunchy catalogue of 'Numbers' banned by the BBC?

10. *Pieces Of Eight* was a 1978 album by which AOR act?

11. 'Seven Seas Of Rhye' gave Queen their first a) Top 30 b) Top 20 c) Top 10 hit?

12. The Who caught the 5:15 train, presumably to Brighton, in which year?

13. 'Three Times A Lady' was a transatlantic Number 1 for The Commodores, but who wrote it?

14. Which hip hop firebrands claimed '911 Is A Joke'?

15. Which hugely successful AOR act called out 'Hey Nineteen' in 1980?

THE OFFSPRING

Sons and daughters of the famous…

1. Which British rock frontman eventually acknowledged parentage of singer and actress Marsha Hunt's daughter Karis?

2. Despite claiming that their first-born would be called God, Grace Slick and Paul Kantner's daughter was eventually named after a country. Which one?

3. Julian Lennon made his public entrance with which single in 1984?

4. Jeff Buckley prepared for fleeting fame with the help of which one-time member of Captain Beefheart's Magic Band?

5. Though she sings, Marvin Gaye's daughter is now better known for her acting career. Who is she?

6. Which of Bob Dylan's sons recorded a version of John Lennon's 'Gimme Some Truth' with George Harrison's son Dhani?

7. Which McCartney daughter is now an acclaimed photographer?

8. Which scion of Frank Zappa joined him in 1982 to sing the dubious praises of the 'Valley Girl'?

9. Born in 1971, Zowie Bowie is now a celebrated film director and better known by which name?

10. Tim Buckley's son Jeff sang his way to instant acclaim on his 1994 album, *Grace*. But what was the title of its two-disc follow-up, released in 1998 a year after his death?

11. Kirsty MacColl's father was the folksinging legend Ewan MacColl. He also wrote a love ballad that in 1972 became a huge hit for Roberta Flack. What was it called?

12. Which cult 1980s singer named his son, now a model, Jethro in honour of the blues rock-turned-prog outfit Jethro Tull?

13. Liv Tyler is the daughter of Aerosmith frontman Steven Tyler. Who's her mum?

14. While better known as the wife of Ozzy Osbourne, Sharon Osbourne is the daughter of which notorious British rock manager and agent, the self styled 'Al Capone of Pop'?

15. Rufus Wainwright is the nephew of one of the McGarrigle sisters. Which one?

OUT OF THE BLUE: 15 UNLIKELY HIT SINGLES

Here's the song. Now name the artist...

1. 'O Superman'

2. 'I Feel Love'

3. 'Playground Twist'

4. 'Hocus Pocus'

5. 'Theme From *Shaft*'

6. 'Mouldy Old Dough'

7. 'Death Disco'

8. 'Rockit'

9. 'Silver Machine'

10. 'Money' (1979 version)

11. 'Rock On'

12. 'Rock Lobster'

13. 'Lucky Number'

14. '19'

15. 'Autobahn'

PARTNERS

1. Who married Jim Kerr in 1984?

2. Rod Stewart's mid-1970s squeeze, Britt Ekland, was previously married to which British comedy actor?

3. Who was the male half of Everything But The Girl?

4. In 1964, Marvin Gaye married the 37-year old sister of Motown boss Berry Gordy. Who was she?

5. What age was Bill Wyman when he married his teenage sweetheart Mandy Smith a) 48 b) 52 c) 56

6. Rita Coolidge was married to which actor turned singer songwriter?

7. After splitting from Adam Ant, which actress went on to greater fame in the 1980s, starring in films such as *Castaway*?

8. She was the subject of love songs by both Country Joe McDonald and Leonard Cohen. Who was she?

9. Stevie Wonder was briefly married to which Motown singer-songwriter?

10. Which famous other half later wrote two books on her rock 'n' roll past – *Free Spirit* and *Backstage Passes*?

11. Who was the *Diary of a Mad Housewife* actress and early 1970s partner of Neil Young?

12. Prior to her relationship with Mick Jagger, Marianne Faithfull was married to which influential London counterculture figure?

13. Johnny Cash and June Carter married in a) 1964 b) 1966 c) 1968?

14. Jim Morrison's lover found him dead in the bath. Who was she?

15. Which member of the Banshees did singer Siouxsie end up marrying?

PLACES

Who sang about the following locations?

1. 'Baker Street'

2. 'Rio'

3. 'LA Woman'

4. 'West End Girls'

5. 'Midnight Train To Georgia'

6. 'Vienna'

7. 'Warszawa'

8. 'Solsbury Hill'

9. '(White Man) In Hammersmith Palais'

10. 'Copenhagen'

11. 'Bron-Y-Aur Stomp'

12. 'Streets Of London'

13. 'The Wall Street Shuffle'

14. 'Echo Beach'

15. 'New Amsterdam'

POLITICS

1. Which punk band released a campaigning single on behalf of Liddle Towers, who died shortly after leaving police custody in 1976?

2. Which band advised the then Prime Minister to 'Stand Down Margaret'?

3. 1971 saw Bob Dylan release acoustic and electric versions of a politically charged 45 named after a black political activist killed in a prison shootout in California. Who was he?

4. Which act didn't contribute to the consciousness-raising 1985 anthem 'Sun City', credited to Artists United Against Apartheid a) Pat Benatar b) Queen c) Bruce Springsteen?

5. Band Aid, Live Aid and 'Do They Know It's Christmas?' dominated the pop landscape during 1984–1985. But who was the BBC television journalist whose reports from Ethiopia first inspired Bob Geldof into action?

6. Which bunch of Bristol-based firebrands released an extraordinary single-sized tirade against capitalism in 1979 titled 'We Are All Prostitutes'?

7. The Specials bowed out in 1981 with 'Ghost Town', about the social ills associated with unemployment. Which city did the band call home?

8. Who wrote 'Give Ireland Back To The Irish', a 1972 Top 20 hit in Britain despite a radio ban?

9. Helen Reddy's feminist anthem 'I Am Woman' topped the US singles chart (and failed to register in Britain) in which year?

10. 'Student Demonstration Time' was a rare incursion into protest rock by which US group?

11. Sugarhill Gang's 'Rapper's Delight' was confirmation that rap was every bit as much the voice of the dispossessed as punk had been a few years earlier. At the end of which year did it enter the British chart?

12. Which post-punk band sang about torture and injustice in the *OGWT* studio via their 1981 song 'Armagh'?

13. Which band debuted in 1979 with 'California Uber Alles', a blistering attack on the corrupting influence of power?

14. Who was the Yippie activist who interrupted The Who's performance at Woodstock?

15. Politically conscious hip hop legend Carlton Ridenhour is better known as...?

POST-PUNK

1. Which summer 1979 festival held in Leeds was billed as 'the world's first science fiction rock 'n' roll extravaganza'?

2. 'Paris Maquis' by Metal Urbain was the debut single on which key post-punk independent record label?

3. Cabaret Voltaire took their name from a) a Dada club in First World War Zurich b) a Nazi club in 1920s Berlin c) a secret group of Enlightenment intellectuals in 18th-century Paris?

4. Oxford Road Show television presenter and Nico biographer Richard 'Dick' Witts fronted which Manchester post-punk outfit?

5. The sleeve of Bow Wow Wow's 1981 debut *See Jungle! See Jungle!* ... album, was based on a painting by a French Impressionist artist. Who was he?

6. Guitarist Brix Smith joined The Fall in time for the making of which album?

7. The Cure's debut single, 'Killing An Arab', took its inspiration from a classic existentialist novel written by whom?

8. Which apocalyptic, anti-rock noise quartet debuted late in 1977 with an album titled *Second Annual Report*?

9. The Slits' first album, 1979's *Cut*, was produced by which dub reggae artist?

10. After the success of her 1982 debut album, *Big Science*, and its follow-up, *Mister Heartbreak*, Laurie Anderson took the extraordinary step of releasing a five-disc live collection. What was it called?

11. Which band announced their arrival with the 1979 single 'She Is Beyond Good And Evil'?

12. Swiss all-woman post-punk quartet Kleenex were obliged to change their name… to what?

13. Which Leeds-based band debuted with a three-track EP titled *Damaged Goods*?

14. Who posed the question 'Where's Captain Kirk'?

15. Which post-punk duo's debut album bore the title *We Buy A Hammer For Daddy*?

PRE-PUNK

1. John Cale famously produced The Stooges' debut. But who was the man behind the controls for the New York Dolls' inaugural set?

2. The seeds of Television were sown when Richard 'Hell' Meyers and Tom 'Verlaine' Miller formed which three-piece band in autumn 1972?

3. Who was the one-time Warhol associate who later managed Johnny Thunders and The Heartbreakers (and take care over the spelling of his first name)?

4. The New York Dolls' drummer died during the band's visit to London in November 1972. Who was he?

5. CBGB's in New York is often cited as the venue that launched punk rock. But what did its full name CBGB & OMFUG stand for?

6. Which ballsy San Francisco band invited the world to 'Shake Some Action' in 1976?

7. Neu!'s prototype punk song 'Hero' was released on which album?

8. Malcolm McLaren and Vivienne Westwood's cultish Kings Road fashion hideaway opened late in 1971 as a) SEX b) Too Fast To Live, Too Young To Die c) Let It Rock

9. What was the title of Dr. Feelgood's mid-1970s

debut album?

10. Which journalist turned guitarist wrote about 'punk rock' in his sleeve notes for the 1972 garage band compilation *Nuggets*?

11. Which underground band's 1971 song 'Do It' was virtually a template for punk rock action?

12. For which album did Lou Reed record 'Vicious'?

13. The Joe Strummer-fronted pub rockers The 101'ers enjoyed a nine-month residency at which West London pub?

14. What was the name of the Detroit venue where the MC5 recorded their classic 1969 *Kick Out The Jams* album?

15. Who were the original British 'numbskull' band, a reputation enhanced by mid-1960s hits such as 'Wild Thing' and 'I Can't Control Myself'?

PRESLEY SEVENTIES

During the last decade of his life, Elvis handpicked numerous classics and instant standards…

1. Who was the first to record 'Always On My Mind'?

2. 'Amazing Grace' was a 1970 hit for which US singer?

3. Which British pop balladeer had a hit in 1967 with 'There Goes My Everything'?

4. Whose 1971 arrangement of 'An American Trilogy' did Elvis base his version on?

5. 'And I Love You So' was a 1970 cut written by which emerging singer?

6. 'The Impossible Dream' as originally written for which mid-1960s musical?

7. Who wrote 'Early Morning Rain'?

8. It was, said Elvis of this Hank Williams original, the saddest song he'd ever heard.

9. R&B singer Arthur Alexander was the first to release which 1972 Presley A-side?

10. 'Proud Mary' was a concert favourite of Presley's during the first years of his comeback. Who wrote it?

11. Buffy Sainte-Marie was the writer of which 1972 Presley hit?

12. 'Help Me Make It Through The Night' was first written and recorded by which singer turned actor?

13. 'Make The World Go Away' first appeared on which Presley album?

14. Which country singer wrote 'You Gave Me A Mountain'?

15. Before Elvis got hold of it, 'It's Impossible' had been a 1970 hit for which smooth balladeer?

PRODUCERS

1. Which producer was brought in to salvage the Beatles' *Let It Be* tapes?

2. Who was the independently spirited producer-boss of Elektra Records?

3. Cult 1960s psychedelic act the Red Crayola returned in the late 1970s, after which the band's main man became an in-house producer at Rough Trade Records. Who was he?

4. A veteran rock producer best known for his work with Blue Oyster Cult was drafted in to give The Clash's second album, *Give 'Em Enough Rope*, some US-friendly punch. Who was he?

5. Whose groundbreaking early and mid-1970s productions were forged in a studio he called the Black Ark?

6. Hard rock and metal producer Mutt Lange was married to which Canadian singer for over a decade?

7. Which West Coast pop impresario produced Carole King's 1971 *Tapestry* album?

8. What was Jimmy Miller's first album project with the Rolling Stones?

9. Who managed to tame the Sex Pistols for long enough to get *Never Mind The Bollocks* ... in the can?

10. It took two acolytes to nail Lou Reed's *Transformer*. Who were they?

11. It wasn't always easy going, but XTC's *Skylarking* certainly benefited from the input of which pop magician?

12. The label boss was so enthused at having signed the B-52's that he produced their debut himself. Who was he?

13. The Hi Records boss was not going to let anyone else near the controls while getting Al Green's 'Let's Stay Together' in the bag.

14. Who else could have masterminded the soulful, tripped-out production of Funkadelic's *Maggot Brain* but the man himself?

15. Miles Davis's long-time producer was there again for the groundbreaking *Bitches Brew*.

PROG

1.   When keyboard player Rick Wakeman joined Yes in 1971, it ushered in the band's classic era. Who did he replace?

2.   In 1973, Arthur Brown's Kingdom Come released an album that featured a Bentley Rhythm Ace drum machine. What was the title?

3.   The Mahavishnu Orchestra's *Birds Of Fire* album opens with the sound of a) a loud gong b) a sharp intake of breath c) a quiet singing bell?

4.   Gong's 'Radio Gnome' trilogy of albums began with *Flying Teapot* and ended with *You*. What was the middle set called?

5.   Asia were an early 1980s supergroup made up of ex-members from King Crimson (John Wetton), Emerson, Lake & Palmer (Carl Palmer) and Yes (Steve Howe). Who was the ex-member of Buggles that made up the quartet?

6.   Van Der Graaf Generator frontman Peter Hammill a) moonlighted as a writer for US rock magazine *Rolling Stone* b) wrote a song inspired by British actress Susan Penhaligon c) is the scion of a great British inventor?

7.   Gentle Giant, who formed around the nucleus of the three Shulman brothers, grew out of which late-1960s psychedelic showband?

8.   Pete Sinfield, King Crimson lyricist and producer

of the first Roxy Music album, released his own album in 1973. What was it called?

9.   Demis Roussos fronted these Greek prog-rockers and played the bass. Vangelis handled the keyboards. Who were they?

10. While on his way out from Soft Machine, Robert Wyatt released his first solo album. The title?

11. Keith Emerson arrived via The Nice and Greg Lake from King Crimson. But what was ELP drummer Carl Palmer's previous band?

12. Who yodelled his way through Focus's surprise 1973 progressive rock hit 45 'Hocus Pocus'?

13. Where, in May 1975, did Rick Wakeman mount his disastrous 'King Arthur on ice' shows?

14. Years after their mid-1970s prime, Yes scored a US Number 1 single in 1984 with which song?

15. Pompeii was the atmospheric location in October 1971 for a concert-style film, released the following year, featuring which progressive rock notables?

PROG ROCK ON 45

Unlikely three-minute heroes – but who were they?

1. 'The Knife'

2. 'Sympathy'

3. 'Theme One'

4. 'Back Street Luv'

5. 'Question'

6. 'Roundabout'

7. 'Nut Rocker'

8. 'Bungle In The Jungle'

9. 'Hocus Pocus'

10. 'Hold Your Head Up'

11. 'Joybringer'

12. 'Tomorrow Night'

13. 'Burlesque'

14. 'Celebration'

15. 'Conquistador'

PUNK

1. Who was not a member of the Bromley Contingent? a) David Bowie b) Billy Idol c) Siouxsie Sioux

2. *Sniffin' Glue* is the best-known punk fanzine. But what was its full name?

3. John Holmstrom founded the influential New York fanzine *Punk*. He also illustrated the cartoon cover for which 1978 Ramones album?

4. Malcolm McLaren and Vivienne Westwood had SEX. But which Kings Road punk boutique was set up by John Krivine?

5. Late in 1976, a basement club opened in Liverpool to cater for punk and new wave bands just spitting distance away from the Cavern. What was it called?

6. What was the title of an early punk single released by Australian band The Saints?

7. Who in 1978 ranted about 'Fulham Fallout'?

8. Too much even for most punk audiences, these Industrial music pioneers famously declared, 'Rock is for arse-lickers.' Who were they?

9. After producing demos for the Sex Pistols, guitarist Chris Spedding briefly teamed up with which R&B-turned-punk combo, veterans of the September 1976 100 Club Punk Rock Festival?

10. Who starred in Derek Jarman's punk film *Jubilee* before launching her solo career in 1979 with *Sheep Farming In Barnet*?

11. Which punk band took their name from a phrase they spotted in a review of TV musical drama *Rock Follies*?

12. Which future punk starlet started out as an aspiring pop-reggae singer known as Mari Elliott?

13. The Adverts made a memorable appearance on *Top of the Pops* in 1977 performing which song?

14. Which band's early catchphrase was 'Gabba Gabba Hey'?

15. Who played guitar on The Damned's debut album?

PUNK ON FIRE

This lot weren't afraid to spit it out... Who were they?

1. 'Complete Control'
2. 'In A Rut'
3. 'God Save The Queen'
4. 'Borstal Breakout'
5. 'Oh Bondage Up Yours!'
6. 'New Town'
7. 'How Much Longer'
8. 'Playground Twist'
9. 'Where Were You?'
10. 'Shot By Both Sides'
11. 'Goodbye Toulouse'
12. 'Nobody's Scared'
13. 'Final Solution'
14. 'New Rose'
15. 'One Chord Wonders'

RADIO

1. What was the name of John Peel's 1967 psychedelic radio show broadcast by the offshore pirate Radio London?

2. Who was the self-styled 'Hairy Cornflake'?

3. Simon Dee began his broadcasting career at which pirate radio station?

4. In which month and year did the BBC launch Radio One?

5. Which Carpenters single begins with a conversation between a radio DJ and an alien?

6. Who released the 'Radio Radio' single in 1978?

7. During the mid-1990s, a massive purge of the Radio One old guard saw the station reposition itself towards a young audience. Who was the Controller responsible?

8. Which eclectic and influential Radio 1 DJ was affectionately known as 'Fluff'?

9. Which 1974 Harry Chapin hit concerned the plight of an ageing DJ?

10. Who was John Peel's long-standing and highly influential Radio One producer?

11. Which DJ, a pal of The Beatles and an artful tape manipulator, was sacked both by Radio London and Radio One during a gloriously

controversial career?

12. Whose Radio One *Friday Rock Show* did much to popularise the hard rock and metal revival of the 1980s?

13. What was the name of Tony Blackburn's dog?

14. BBC Radio cult hero and ex-Fall guitarist Marc Riley once fronted his own band. Who were they?

15. Which Radio One DJ sparked a furore by refusing to play Frankie Goes To Hollywood's 'Relax'?

REGGAE

1. This Jamaican band's 1970 single 'Pressure Drop' was later covered by The Clash. Who were they?

2. Though UB40 based their hit version of 'Red Red Wine' on Tony Tribe's mid-1970s reggae rendition, the song was originally written and released in 1968 by which production-line hitmaker?

3. Who, early in 1978, topped the British singles chart with 'Uptown Top Ranking'?

4. Which dub producer was behind Janet Kay's 1978 hit 'Silly Games'?

5. Who in 1982 invited us to 'Pass The Dutchie'?

6. Which trio commemorated the arrival of 1977 with the *Two Sevens Clash* album?

7. *King Tubby[s] Meets Rockers Uptown* from 1976 was a breakthrough set for which melodica-playing reggae legend?

8. Which Birmingham-based reggae act enjoyed a hit crossover album in 1978 with *Handsworth Revolution*?

9. By which name is Winston Rodney better known?

10. 'Money in My Pocket' was a 1979 hit for which reggae showman?

11. Burning Spear paid tribute to which Jamaican thinker and activist with which 1975 album?

12. Who was known as the Cool Ruler?

13. Bass Culture was the classic work of which homegrown dub poet?

14. Which pioneering South London MC emerged with the 'Cockney Translation' single in 1984?

15. Who was the *Cry Tuff Dub Encounter* dubmaster?

REVIVE 45

The early to mid 1970s witnessed a revival in vintage pop. Which artists saw these old chestnuts return to the charts?

1. 'Leader Of The Pack'

2. 'Itchycoo Park'

3. 'Space Oddity'

4. 'Oh Carol'

5. 'Sweet Talkin' Guy'

6. 'Nut Rocker'

7. 'My Guy'

8. 'The Loco-Motion'

9. 'I Get The Sweetest Feeling'

10. 'Hi-Ho Silver Lining'

11. 'Shotgun Wedding'

12. 'Nights In White Satin'

13. 'Ying Tong Song'

14. 'Monster Mash'

15. 'The Laughing Gnome'

THE ROCK INVASION

At the time that *OGWT* was being hatched, numerous rock tunes were finding their way into the singles chart. Name the acts responsible…

1. 'Witch's Promise' / 'Teacher'

2. 'I'm A Man'

3. 'Let's Work Together'

4. 'House Of The Rising Sun'

5. 'Brontosaurus'

6. 'The Green Manalishi'

7. 'All Right Now'

8. 'Strange Band'

9. 'Black Night'

10. 'Paranoid'

11. 'Voodoo Chile'

12. 'Whole Lotta Love'

13. 'Jig A Jig'

14. 'Devil's Answer'

15. 'Back Street Luv'

ROCK 'N' ROLL

1. Link Wray's hit instrumental from 1958 sounded so menacing that it prompted a ban by several US radio stations. What was its title?

2. Phil Spector produced the 1975 album *Born To Be With You* for which Bronx-born rock 'n' roll veteran?

3. In 1986, guitarist Duane Eddy teamed up with which electro-pop act for a successful revival of his old 'Peter Gunn' hit?

4. A bobbysoxxer teen idol returned in 1972 with a singer-songwriter-style hit, 'Garden Party'. Who was he?

5. Which homegrown rock 'n' roller plays Stormy Tempest in the 1973 revival film *That'll Be The Day*?

6. Marty Wilde's son was a teen mag favourite during the early 1970s. What was his name?

7. Chantilly Lace almost scraped a top 30 placing in 1972 for which legendary rock 'n' roller?

8. Which late-1950s vocal group returned to the British charts in 1972 with a revival of their mid-1960s single 'Come On Over To My Place'?

9. An early 1980s rock 'n' roll revival trio had a transatlantic hit with 'Rock This Town'. Who were they?

10. The Father of Rock 'n' Roll, Bill Haley died in a) 1975 b) 1979 c) 1981

11. After the success of 'My Ding-A-Ling', spring 1973 saw Chuck Berry return to the British singles chart with which song?

12. MC5 and Roy Wood attracted boos and worse at the London Rock 'n' Roll Show held at Wembley Stadium in 1972. The reason? a) They were late on stage b) They had long hair c) They were rubbish

13. Who sang affectionately in 1977 of 'Sweet Gene Vincent'?

14. Rough mixes of John Lennon's *Rock 'n' Roll* album were briefly made available via mail order. What was the title of the hastily withdrawn album?

15. Before scoring with their electro take on 'Money', the Flying Lizards debuted with a version of which Eddie Cochran hit?

SESSION MEN

1. Which legendary session musician made a rare foray centre-stage with an all-star 1973 album titled *The Tin Man Was A Dreamer*?

2. The Funk Brothers are associated with which legendary label?

3. He's played with John Lennon, Pink Floyd and Paul Simon, amongst numerous others. And he's often wielding a 'stick' bass. Who is he?

4. Which popular session musician co-wrote 'Grandad', the winter 1970 hit for actor Clive Dunn?

5. Who is the busy percussionist often seen performing on stage with Elton John and Eric Clapton?

6. Which legendary bassist was a key member of the Wrecking Crew, Los Angeles' hotshot team of session players who played on numerous Phil Spector, Beach Boys and Monkees sessions?

7. Session drummer Jim Keltner has worked with all of the solo Beatles except one. Who?

8. Which in-demand drummer played on both Sly And The Family Stone's *Fresh* and John Lennon's *Double Fantasy*?

9. This session drummer's journey during the 1970s and early 1980s took him from Roy Ayers and

David Bowie to Stevie Wonder. Who is he?

10.   Who was the bassist for most of Motown's 1960s and early 1970s sessions?

11.   Having backed numerous singer-songwriters, including Stevie Nicks, James Taylor, Warren Zevon and Linda Ronstadt, which illustrious session player was brought on board as second guitarist in Keith Richards X-Pensive Winos project?

12.   Which hugely rated percussionist also had a prominent solo career during the 1980s thanks to the support of Prince?

13.   Who played piano on 'Bridge Over Troubled Water', bass on 'Mr. Tambourine Man' and was a member of Bread?

14.   Which future member of Led Zeppelin arranged strings on the Rolling Stones' 'She's A Rainbow'?

15.   During the early 1970s, session guitarist Albert Lee briefly led his own band. Who were they?

SINGER-SONGWRITERS

1. Which nerve-wracked young singer-songwriter was booed off stage at the 1967 Monterey Pop Festival?

2. The most successful singer-songwriter album of the early 1970s included James Taylor and Joni Mitchell in the credits and was billed as being 'hand stitched' in ads. What was it?

3. What is the connection between the 1964 hit 'World Without Love' and James Taylor?

4. Whose third album for Elektra, issued in 1972, was titled *American Gothic*?

5. Art Garfunkel took the title for his 1973 solo album, *Angel Clare*, from a character in which Thomas Hardy novel?

6. Which British singer-songwriter poured his observations gained from working in institutions into his harrowing 1971 debut album, *Case History*?

7. Whose *Songs For The Gentle Man* was released on John Peel's Dandelion label in 1971?

8. Paul Simon appeared in which Woody Allen film?

9. What was the title of Donovan's 1973 comeback album?

10. *Time Of The Last Persecution* was greeted with virtual silence on its release in 1971. Now, of course, its architect is a weird-folk cult hero. Who was he?

11. Who in 1985 sang wistfully of 'Marlene On The Wall'?

12. Nilsson had the hit, but who wrote 'Everybody's Talkin"?

13. Which singer-songwriter volunteered '50 Ways To Leave Your Lover' in 1975?

14. Melanie's 'Brand New Key' was reworked as 'Combine Harvester', a 1976 chart-topper for which group of English cider-drinkers?

15. Who fronted Planxty before embarking on a solo career in 1975?

SONGS ABOUT STARS AND STARDOM

Who performed...

1. 'Gonna Make You A Star'

2. 'Highway Star'

3. 'Star Star' (alias 'Starfucker')

4. 'Lady Stardust'

5. 'Everybody Is A Star'

6. 'Wishing On A Star'

7. 'Starpower'

8. 'Another Star'

9. 'Evening Star' (the rock song)

10. 'I'm In Love With A German Film Star'

11. 'Dark Star'

12. 'Shooting Star'

13. 'Superstar' (the MOR hit)

14. 'Video Killed The Radio Star'

15. 'Star Trekkin''

SONGS ABOUT TRAVEL

Who performed...

1. '2-4-6-8 Motorway'

2. 'On The Road Again'

3. 'Love Train'

4. 'The Back Seat Of My Car'

5. 'Born To Run'

6. 'Run To Me'

7. 'Float On'

8. 'On The Run'

9. 'Speed King'

10. 'Fast Cars'

11. 'Life In The Fast Lane'

12. 'Up The Ladder To The Roof'

13. 'Papa Was A Rollin' Stone'

14. 'I'll Fly For You'

15. 'Crosstown Traffic'

SOUL

1. What was the title of Billy Paul's 1973 hit song about an extramarital fling?

2. Which vocal group went out 'Walking In The Rain With The One I Love' in 1972?

3. Which of the three Isley Brothers delivered the remarkable, Hendrix-inspired lead guitar break on the band's 1973 hit 'That Lady'?

4. Almost a decade after his 1965 hit 'The "In" Crowd', Dobie Gray returned to the US singles chart in 1973 with which much-loved hit?

5. What, in the name of the 1974 hit for MFSB And The Three Degrees, was 'TSOP'?

6. 'Little' Esther Phillips had a 1972 R&B chart hit with the gritty drug song 'Home Is Where The Hatred Is', but who wrote it?

7. Who in 1985 was riding up the 'Freeway Of Love'?

8. Chaka Khan came to prominence in 1974 fronting her band Rufus and hitting the US Top 3 with which single?

9. Who was Al Green's mentor at Hi Records?

10. Which ex-Temptations singer hit Number 1 in the US singles chart in 1973 with 'Keep On Truckin"?

11. Her voice helped The Crusaders' 'Street Life' become an enormous hit in 1979, after which she took off on a solo career, even scoring a hit with a version of Bob Dylan's 'Knocking On Heaven's Door'. Who is she?

12. Who in 1971s was the 'Clean Up Woman'?

13. What was the title of Bobby Womack's acclaimed 1981 comeback album?

14. 1972's 'Papa Was A Rolling Stone' was a triumph of psychedelic soul and a hit for which fast-changing Motown act?

15. 'Geno' by Dexys Midnight Runners was a homage to Geno Washington. What was the name of the soul legend's late-1960s backing band?

SOUNDTRACKS

1. Who was the man behind the 1971 *Sweet Sweetback's Baadasssss Song* film and soundtrack?

2. Which 1973 George Lucas film was a hits-filled coming-of-age glimpse of small-town 1950s USA?

3. Obscure Italian prog-era act Goblin provided added spookiness on which Dario Argento-directed chiller from 1976?

4. Whose haunting slide guitar evoked the strange vastness of the landscape on Wim Wenders' 1984 film *Paris, Texas*?

5. Who scored numerous Sergio Leone Spaghetti Westerns during the 1960s?

6. Lalo Schifrin scored which classic series of action films?

7. Carly Simon's 1977 hit 'Nobody Does It Better' was the theme to which film?

8. Bacharach and David's 'Raindrops Keep Fallin' On My Head' was written for the 1969 film *Butch Cassidy and the Sundance Kid*. Who had the US Number 1 hit with it?

9. Phil Collins wrote, sang and had great success with a theme song for which 1984 film, directed by Taylor Hackford?

10. Which Francis Ford Coppola musical from 1982 was scored by Tom Waits?

11. Who did the soundtrack for the 1973 blaxploitation film *Black Caesar*?

12. Which Fred Neil song became a huge hit for Harry Nilsson thanks to its appearance on the *Midnight Cowboy* soundtrack?

13. Randy Newman's 'Gone Dead Train' appeared on the soundtrack to which latterly acclaimed British crime thriller?

14. Which Badfinger song was used as the theme for the 1969 film comedy *The Magic Christian*?

15. Whose 'Freddie's Dead' was subtitled 'Theme From *Superfly*' on the 1972 single release?

SPACE SONGS

1. Hawkwind's *In Search Of Space* boasted a fold-out cover designed by who?

2. 'Space Monkey' was a 1978 album track by the so-called 'High Priestess of Rebellion'. Who was she?

3. One of the late 1970s great disco 45s was 'Spacer', penned by the Chic team, but who was the single credited to?

4. Which band had their own Inner Space studio?

5. One of the great post-punk bands released a spooky, dub-inspired single, 'Animal Space'. Who were they?

6. On which Yes album did 'Starship Trooper' first appear?

7. What was the title of Yoko Ono's 1973 album of overtly feminist songs?

8. From which country did Venus hitmakers Shocking Blue hail?

9. Sparks' career was revived in 1979 with an electro-pop set, *No 1 In Heaven*, with a production assist from who?

10. Which late 1960s Grateful Dead celestial epic, which they continued to play for most of their career, could go on for an hour or more?

11. Though many know Don McLean's 1972 hit follow-up to 'American Pie' as 'Starry Starry Night', its proper title is what?

12. 1975 saw the release of whose *Mothership Connection* album?

13. Which 1980 single by Hot Chocolate was apparently inspired by a UFO sighting?

14. 'Flying Saucer Attack' and 'Destination Venus' were both singles by which new wave act?

15. One-hit wonders Space hit Number 2 in 1977 with what song?

THE STONES' SECRETS

But from which album?

1. 'Moonlight Mile'

2. 'Slave'

3. 'Happy'

4. 'Memory Motel'

5. 'Sway'

6. 'Hot Stuff'

7. 'Monkey Man'

8. 'Star Star'

9. 'Hey Negrita'

10. 'Mannish Boy'

11. 'Shine A Light'

12. 'Hand Of Fate'

13. 'Midnight Rambler' (studio version)

14. 'Silver Train'

15. 'Hang Fire'

TEENAGE KICKS

Who released the following odes to teenagerdom?

1. 'Judy Teen'

2. 'Teenage Head'

3. 'Bored Teenagers'

4. '7 Teen'

5. 'Teenage Rampage'

6. 'Teen Age Riot'

7. 'Teenage Wildlife'

8. 'Teenage Lament '74'

9. 'Teenage Lobotomy'

10. 'Teenage Dream'

11. 'Teenage Lust'

12. 'Sixteen'

13. 'I Was A Teenage Werewolf'

14. 'Teenage Depression'

15. 'At Seventeen'

THAT'S MY RECORD!

Name the artist

1. *Hasten Down The Wind*

2. *Night Nurse*

3. *Out Of The Cellar*

4. *Zoot Allures*

5. *Avalon*

6. *Tres Hombres*

7. *Welcome*

8. *Wild Planet*

9. *Islands*

10. *Riptide*

11. *The Silent Corner And The Empty Stage*

12. *Winter In America*

13. *Zen Arcade*

14. *One Nation Under A Groove*

15. *The Colour Of Spring*

THEY WROTE THE SONGS

1.   'Without You'

2.   'People Get Ready'

3.   'Annie's Song'

4.   'Evil Woman' (the mid-1970s hit)

5.   'The Man Who Sold The World'

6.   'Say Say Say'

7.   'Nothing Compares 2 U'

8.   'Hallelujah'

9.   'Both Sides Now'

10. 'Frankly, Mr Shankly'

11. 'Candle In The Wind'

12. 'Come Dancing'

13. 'Stayin' Alive'

14. 'Superstition'

15. 'Hot Love'

TV

1. If Cathy McGowan was the face of *Ready, Steady, Go!*, who was its voice of middle-aged respectability?

2. Channel 4's *The Tube* was broadcast from a studio in which British city?

3. Granada TV's *So It Goes* was hosted by which future record label boss?

4. Which precursor to *OGWT* ran from mid 1968 to mid 1969 and boasted performances by The Move and the Small Faces?

5. Who were the *Top of the Pops* dance troupe before the arrival of Pan's People in 1968?

6. 'Idiot Box' was a savage attack on US group Television by which British punk band?

7. Which ex-member of The Monkees developed a TV programme idea that was later transformed into MTV?

8. The last issue of the *Sniffin' Glue* fanzine included a free flexidisc featuring editor Mark P's new band. Who were they?

9. Which band insisted in 1985 that 'The Sun Always Shines On TV'?

10. Which hip hop act complained in 1988 that 'She Watch Channel Zero?!'?

11. Who duetted with Roger Waters on 'Watching TV' from the ex-Floyd man's 1992 *Amused To Death* album?

12. The Beatles' 'All You Need Is Love' was premiered on which history-making, satellite-linked global broadcast?

13. John Belushi and Dan Aykroyd's Blues Brothers started life on which popular US television show?

14. Which punk band sang 'Television's Over'?

15. Who scored a British Top 30 hit in 1977 with 'Prove It'?

WEST COAST

1.   In 1969, Quicksilver Messenger Service extended an old Bo Diddley number into a side-long psychedelic epic. What was it?

2.   Who was the young, gifted guitarist in Country Joe And The Fish?

3.   Which Captain Beefheart album contained his near mainstream rock classic, 'Big Eyed Beans From Venus'?

4.   Paul Kantner launched the Jefferson Starship name with a 1970 concept album that posited the idea of hippies launching into space and finding peace in another world. What was its title?

5.   After Jim Morrison's death in July 1971, The Doors released two further early 1970s albums, *Other Voices* and which last title?

6.   Jefferson Airplane drummer, Moby Grape guitarist, cult hero extraordinaire, Skip Spence released one solo album in 1969. What was it called?

7.   Who was Randy California's drumming stepdad in Spirit?

8.   Who was the lead guitarist with Jefferson Airplane?

9.   The Grateful Dead's non-playing lyricist Robert

Hunter released his first solo album in 1974. What was it called?

10. Arguably the finest West Coast all-star album was *Rolling Thunder*, released in 1972. Who was the man that brought Garcia, Lesh, Slick, Kantner, et al together?

11. Twiggy's 1976 hit 'Here I Go Again' was written by which countercultural firebrand?

12. What was the name of Janis Joplin's last touring band?

13. Who wrote Love's *Forever Changes* classic, 'Alone Again Or'?

14. Whose 1967 self-titled debut album yielded no less than five singles?

15. Who was The Doors' guitarist?

WHISTLING SONGS

Who performed...

1. '(Sittin' On) The Dock Of The Bay'

2. 'Jealous Guy' (original version)

3. 'Daydream'

4. 'Games Without Frontiers'

5. 'Centrefold'

6. 'Harry Irene'

7. 'Me And Julio Down By The Schoolyard'

8. 'Patience'

9. 'Golden Years'

10. 'Two Of Us'

11. 'I Was Kaiser Bill's Batman'

12. 'Wind Of Change'

13. 'The Stranger'

14. 'Always Look On The Bright Side Of Life'

15. 'Bennie And The Jets'

INTERLUDE

THE WHISTLE TEST TEST

1. *The Old Grey Whistle Test* was first broadcast on what date?

2. The *OGWT* theme was the opening bars of 'Stone Fox Chase', a 1970 single released by country rock band Area Code 615. In which southern US city were the group based? (A clue is in their name.)

3. Who was the original *OGWT* producer? a) Robin Nash b) Michael Appleton c) Johnnie Stewart

4. By the early 1980s, the name of the programme had been abbreviated to what?

5. Which 'about town' London magazine, then associated with the underground movement, did Bob Harris co-found in 1968?

6. The first *OGWT* presenter was journalist Richard Williams, a rare champion of Krautrock, Roxy Music and the Velvet Underground at which British rock weekly paper?

7. Bob Harris acquired his 'Bomber' nickname from a) his fondness for bomber jackets b) his unhurried personal demeanour c) a British Second World War RAF Commander

8. When Bob announced that Jefferson Starship's 'Ride The Tiger' would play out to one of the programme's animated clips, he couldn't quite

pronounce the band's new young lead guitarist's name properly. Who was he?

9. Prior to sitting on the *OGWT* sofa, Andy Kershaw was roadie for which British singer? a) Bryan Ferry b) Kevin Coyne c) Billy Bragg

10. During the early 1970s, Harris was also a regular presenter on which late night Radio One programme that specialised in album-oriented rock?

11. In what year did Bob Harris leave *OGWT*?

12. Who replaced him?

13. Which *OGWT* presenter played alongside ex-British Prime Minister Tony Blair in a short-lived mid-1970s band called Ugly Rumours?

14. Early 1980s *OGWT* co-presenters Mark Ellen and David Hepworth co-founded which successful rock monthly magazine in 1986?

15. Who was Bob Harris's radio mentor?

THE BEST OF THE TEST?

1. The classic PiL line-up that appeared on the Test in 1980 to perform 'Poptones' and 'Careering' from *Metal Box* included which self-taught, dub-inspired bassist?

2. 'Keep On Keeping On', performed live on *OGWT* in 1972, came from Curtis Mayfield's second solo album. What was its title?

3. 'Under My Wheels' was the first single from which Alice Cooper album?

4. The presence of three masked violinists gave the Sensational Alex Harvey Band's rendition of which Jacques Brel song added menace?

5. When Bowie performed Queen Bitch on the show in 1972, was his guitar a) orange b) blue c) pink?

6. Who started off her 1976 performance by uttering the words, 'The time is now,' launched into a ferocious version of the title track of her recent album, then ended her performance with a blissed-out version of 'Hey Joe'?

7. Two album tracks, 'Fan Mail' and 'Detroit 442' sandwiched Blondie's then current single when they appeared on *OGWT* in spring 1978. What was it?

8. The guitarist played a Gibson Firebird. The synth man wore blue eye shadow. And the singer,

like a suave James Cagney, launched into instant classic 'Do The Strand' with the words: 'There's a new sensation!' Who were this great British sensation?

9.   Which all-woman combo was 'Wasted' on *OGWT* in 1977?

10.   Captain Beefheart wasn't at his best for his 1974 *OGWT* appearance. But he was, after all, still Captain Beefheart. What MOR-influenced album was he promoting?

11.   Nico's moody 1974 appearance (with Bob Harris looking visibly bored!) is missing presumed wiped. Which album was she plugging?

12.   One of the most impassioned performances conjured up in the small *OGWT* studio was Tim Buckley's definitive version of 'Dolphins'. Who wrote the song?

13.   Time has not dimmed the insistent energy of Can's 1975 performance of 'Vernal Equinox'. But can you name the hyperactive man in the studded leather jacket karate chopping his keyboard?

14.   The Wailers' frontline of Peter Tosh, Bob Marley and Bunny Wailer mesmerised in 1973 with performances of 'Concrete Jungle' and 'Stir It Up'. But from which album did the songs come?

15.   Focus's British Top 20 hit 'Hocus Pocus', performed on *OGWT* in 1972, features yodelling by the band's flautist and keyboard player. Who was he?

15 SONGS

Who performed...

1. 'Black Coffee' in 1973

2. 'I'm Bored' in 1979

3. 'Sweet Home Alabama' in 1975

4. 'Another Sleep Song' in 1974

5. 'Foxhole' in 1978

6. 'Breadfan' in 1973

7. 'Destination Venus' in 1978

8. 'The Kiss' in 1973

9. 'Inglan Is A Bitch' in 1980

10. 'Short People' in 1978

11. 'Walk Out To Winter' in 1983

12. 'Tiny Dancer' in 1971

13. 'Radios In Motion' in 1978

14. 'Burma Shave' in 1979

15. 'Lorelei' in 1984

WHO SAID WHAT?

1. Introduced his band with the words, 'At last, the 1978 show.'

2. Picked up a phone and said, 'This is the Killer speaking.'

3. 'You can pop yer acid spangle in now – we're gonna do a Rita Coolidge number for ya.'

4. 'Hello there in living room land.'

5. 'Right, here's another piece of completely escapist light entertainment.'

6. 'We'd like to do a song for my mum cos she likes this one.'

7. 'They just said talk about Neil Young, but I don't like to talk about the gentleman.'

8. 'Hands up all the very intelligent people in this living room. [Cheer] Hands up all the stupids. [Bigger cheer]'

9. 'The great strength of heavy metal is that it doesn't progress.'

10. 'Shut up, listen and dance.'

11. Mentions Rolf Harris...

12. 'Would the owner of the blue Ford Cortina registration number PEN 1S please go to reception as it's blocking a fire exit.'

13. 'I'd like to say hello to all the folks in England. How ya doing, folks? Well, here I am in New York singing to ya.'

14. 'You've got time to go out and make cheese on toast on this one.'

15. Let his harmonium, decorated with the word 'Sewer', do the talking for him?

THE OGWT YEARS
1971

1. Janis Joplin has a posthumous US chart-topper with 'Me And Bobby McGee', written by whom?

2. The Doors' lead vocalist is found dead in which European city?

3. Rod Stewart's 'Maggie May' is a huge transatlantic hit. But it is initially released as a double A-side together with a cover of which Tim Hardin song?

4. The Rolling Stones launch their own record label with a collection of recordings made by their late guitarist, Brian Jones, in which North African country? a) Libya b) Algeria c) Morocco

5. Which well-known rock promoter closes down the Fillmores East and West?

6. Isaac Hayes releases two albums, the soundtrack to *Shaft* and which iconic double-album set?

7. Which infamous rock soundtrack double album, which includes orchestral music, comedy routines and a song called 'Penis Dimension', is released by Frank Zappa?

8. Reggae duo Dave and Ansell Collins hit Number 1 in the spring with a song that still gets played on football terraces. What is it?

9. Confirmation of the growing power of the Northern Soul scene comes in the autumn when a revived vocal group song, 'Hey Girl Don't Bother Me', gives a belated Number 1 hit for which US act?

10. 'Johnny Reggae', credited to the Piglets, is yet another 'one-hit wonder' success for which British record producer?

11. James Taylor has the hit with it, but who's the writer of 'You've Got A Friend'?

12. After a ten-year slog, which guitarist from the Southern States is killed in a motorbike accident in October just as his talents are being recognised worldwide?

13. A new band featuring Lowell George, Bill Payne and ex-Mothers Of Invention bassist Roy Estrada release their self titled debut album. Who are they?

14. It features 'Sweet Leaf' and 'Children Of The Grave', it ups the darkness quota and it is Black Sabbath's third album. What is the title?

15. Carole King releases two albums during 1971. The first is *Tapestry*. What's the second?

THE OGWT YEARS
1972

1. Which minor single from 1968 is reissued on the back of T. Rex's 1970s success in the spring and becomes a Top 10 hit?

2. Which US soul singer enjoys a Top 10 hit in Britain during 1972 with 'Let's Stay Together'?

3. Nick Drake's third and final album is released to little fanfare. Title?

4. *Something/Anything* is a remarkable double album by a soloist who sings and plays everything on it. Who is he?

5. This classic live album includes versions of Alvin Lee's 'Hear Me Calling' and Steppenwolf's 'Born To Be Wild'. What is it called?

6. Lou Reed's self-titled debut album includes a track called 'Berlin' but is recorded in a different European capital city. Which one?

7. Pink Floyd's *Obscured By Clouds* soundtrack album is their second collaboration with which film director?

8. John Sinclair, immortalised on John and Yoko's *Some Time In New York City* album, had previously been manager of the MC5 and co-founder of which radical political organisation?

9.　'Guitar Man' vocal group Bread are fronted by a songwriter/producer who worked with Captain Beefheart in the mid 1960s. Who is he?

10.　What is the title of the three-disc live album released in 1972 by the Grateful Dead?

11.　The Edgar Winter Group's *They Only Come Out At Night* includes the band's best-known song, an instrumental and a hit single the following year. What is it called?

12.　Argent, who break through with the hit single 'Hold Your Head Up', are named after keyboard man Rod who was previously a founder member of which 1960s beat group?

13.　Organised by Stax Records, this August 1972 concert, held in Los Angeles and with the Staple Singers and Isaac Hayes heading the bill, is often regarded as the black community's answer to Woodstock. How is the show, later the subject of a documentary, billed?

14.　Just a year after Neil Young writes 'The Needle And The Damage Done', partly as a result of observing heroin addiction at close hand, an errant Crazy Horse guitarist overdoses in November 1972. Who was he?

15.　Jackson Browne becomes one of the first new artists to emerge via David Geffen's new record label with strong sales for his self-titled debut album, released at the start of the year. What is Geffen's trailblazing label?

THE OGWT YEARS
1973

1. 1973 is the best year yet for RAK Records, with Suzi Quatro, Hot Chocolate and Mud emerging as regular hitmakers. But which noted record producer runs the label?

2. It features a prism on the cover and contains some of the most technically accomplished music within its distinctive packaging. It is, of course…?

3. Richard Branson launches Virgin Records with an almost entirely instrumental album by a virtual unknown. What is it?

4. Slade's drummer is badly injured in a car crash. Who is he?

5. Bruce Springsteen's debut album, *Greetings From Asbury Park, N.J.*, includes 'Blinded By The Light', which was quickly covered by Manfred Mann's Earth Band. But who in the mid-1970s recorded but did not release the album's closer, 'It's Hard To Be A Saint In The City'?

6. 'Stuck In The Middle With You' is a hit for which folk-rock outfit?

7. Which 1960s folk-rock pioneers call it a day in 1973 after releasing a lukewarm reunion album?

8. Perhaps the cult British album of the year is *Solid Air*. Who is the artist?

9. A live album, *30 Seconds Over Winterland*, signals the end for which late-1960s acid-rock high flyers?

10. Dylan's hit 'Knockin' On Heaven's Door' is written for which film soundtrack?

11. How many British Top 30 hits are pulled from Stevie Wonder's *Innervisions*? a) 1 b) 2 c) 3

12. Who doesn't play at Eric Clapton's January 1973 Rainbow concert? a) Steve Winwood b) Ronnie Wood c) Roy Wood

13. What is Suzi Quatro's first British hit single?

14. Ike & Tina Turner go out on a high with their last hit single in autumn 1973. What is it?

15. Budgie's most famous track, 'Breadfan', appears on which 1973 album?

THE OGWT YEARS
1974

1. Johnny Winter records two Jagger/Richards songs for his 1973 album, *Still Alive And Well*. He plays a third on a 1974 visit to the *OGWT* studio. What is it?

2. In a key moment in John Lennon's 'Lost Weekend', the ex-Beatle and an American songwriter friend are thrown out of the Troubadour in Los Angeles after some rowdy heckling. Who is Lennon's bearded pal?

3. The year sees ex-Spiders From Mars guitarist and Bowie's main collaborator Mick Ronson produce a first solo album. Title?

4. Humble Pie cover 'I Can't Stand The Rain' on their 1974 *Thunderbox* album, but which American soul singer has the hit with it?

5. If Bowie was Ziggy Stardust, who, in 1974, starts calling himself Zinc Alloy?

6. 'Rikki Don't Lose That Number' is lifted from which Steely Dan album?

7. In which British town does ABBA triumph at the Eurovision Song Contest?

8. Which band, according to their breakthrough album, commit the *Crime Of The Century*?

9. Bowie's *David Live* album is recorded in which soul-fixated US city?

10. Who makes an unexpected appearance in the British singles chart with a cover of the Monkees' 'I'm A Believer'?

11. *Diary of a Rock 'n' Roll Star*, published in the summer, is an account of life on the road by which successful frontman?

12. Which Vinegar Joe singer opts to go solo – which she does with great success – prompting the group to call it a day?

13. Which glam rock band, featuring frontman Michael Des Barres, disband after limited success?

14. The Three Degrees' 'When Will I See You Again' is an enormous success. But who are the two writer/producers behind the hit?

15. Motown artist R. Dean Taylor's Top 3 hit 'There's A Ghost In My House' was first released in a) 1965 b) 1967 c) 1969?

THE OGWT YEARS
1975

1.   A BBC TV documentary about David Bowie, mostly shot during his 1974 US tour, is titled after which Bowie song?

2.   April sees the tragic death of Badfinger's frontman and main songwriter. Who was he?

3.   Jefferson Starship make an unlikely appearance in the US singles chart with which Top 3 hit?

4.   Homegrown Brit-funk arrives in the form of the Average White Band, who follow up their spring hit 'Pick Up The Pieces' with the title track from their summer album. What is it?

5.   The Bay City Rollers' chart-topping 'Bye Bye Baby' was previously a hit in 1965 for which US vocal group?

6.   Which progressive rock bassist enjoys a surprise seasonal hit with 'I Believe In Father Christmas'?

7.   The Bee Gees' renaissance begins with which dancefloor classic?

8.   This is the year that Cher married which US southern rocker?

9.   Which soul star suffers a heart attack on stage in New Jersey that cruelly curtails his career?

10. Tammy Wynette's 'Stand By Your Man' is a British Number 1 in 1975, but had been first released in a) 1958 b) 1968 c) 1971

11. Which glam band emerge from the shadow of their producers with the spring hit, 'Fox On The Run'?

12. Preceded by the hit single 'Down Down', Status Quo release one of the biggest albums of their career in 1975. What is it?

13. 'Lovin' You' is a huge hit for which sweet-voiced US singer?

14. It is the year of the great Dr. Feelgood breakout – but from which distinctive part of the Essex coastline do they hail?

15. *The Original Soundtrack* was not a soundtrack album at all, but the latest successful record by which band?

THE OGWT YEARS
1976

1. What is the first big hit from Peter Frampton's enormously successful *Frampton Comes Alive!* album?

2. Which 1960s trio of pop heart-throbs return with a hit message that reads: 'No Regrets'?

3. Uriah Heep part company with their lead vocalist over his drinking habits. Who is he?

4. 'The Killing Of Georgie' is about the killing of a gay friend of which rock superstar?

5. Which original member of The Supremes dies in February 1976 aged 32?

6. '(Do The) Spanish Hustle' is a British Top 10 hit for which New York disco-funk band?

7. Which uncompromising protest singer takes his own life in April 1976?

8. *Legalise It* is the debut album by which reggae singing legend?

9. 'All By Myself' hitmaker Eric Carmen was previously a member of which early 1970s power pop group?

10. With punk revving up in the undergrowth, which band's *Too Old To Rock 'n' Roll Too Young*

To Die album title seems a little too close for comfort?

11. *Super Ape* turns out to be a hugely influential album by which reggae producer/artist?

12. *Kingfish* is a solo project for which Grateful Dead member?

13. 1976 is the year that the Rolling Stones headline which annual British rock festival?

14. Which top model appears in the video for Bryan Ferry's reworking of Wilbert Harrison's 'Let's Stick Together'?

15. 'Music' is one of the hits of the year for which British musician?

THE OGWT YEARS
1977

1. Who is resident DJ at the Roxy Club, punk rock's leading venue, based in London's Covent Garden?

2. Which New York nightclub opens its doors in the spring?

3. A&M Records press up copies of which projected Sex Pistols single before dropping the band?

4. Elvis Presley is found dead by his model girlfriend. Who is she?

5. Which rock impresario produces the *Saturday Night Fever* film?

6. 1977 sees the release of the first Foreigner album. Who is the band's key songwriter and guitarist?

7. 'Rich Girl' is the first US Number 1 single for which white soul duo?

8. Who quits Genesis, leaving the group to soldier on as a three-piece?

9. Sid Vicious makes his Sex Pistols debut in April 1977 at which North London cinema?

10. Much of the acclaim heaped on Television for

their self-titled debut album is down to the elegant interplay between Tom Verlaine and the band's second guitarist. Who is he?

11. Which rock 'n' roller is eulogised on a single late in the year by Ian Dury?

12. 'Got To Give It Up' is the highest-charting solo single during the 1970s for which artist?

13. The independently released *Spiral Scratch* EP is credited with kick-starting the entire DIY music revolution. The label is New Hormones, but who are the band?

14. In which English county is Solsbury Hill, the subject of Peter Gabriel's first solo single?

15. Which punk band does Marc Bolan take with him on T. Rex's spring tour?

THE OGWT YEARS
1978

1. What is the title of Bob Dylan's four-hour filmed account of his mid-1970s *Rolling Thunder* tour?

2. At the One Love Peace concert in April 1978, Bob Marley brings the leaders of Jamaica's two rival parties together on stage during a performance of a) 'One Love' b) 'Jamming' c) 'I Shot The Sheriff'?

3. The *Sgt Pepper's Lonely Hearts Club Band* film musical also drew on songs from a second Beatles album. Which one?

4. What's the name of Sid Vicious's girlfriend who is found dead in their room at New York's Chelsea Hotel in October?

5. 'I'm Every Woman' is the first solo hit for a singer previously known for her work with US funk band Rufus. Who is she?

6. When found guilty of possessing heroin, Rolling Stone Keith Richards is, as part of his sentence, a) ordered to perform a benefit concert b) ordered to record a benefit album c) ordered out of the country?

7. The newly formed San Francisco punk band Dead Kennedys are fronted by who?

8. Gerry Rafferty's 'Baker Street' is a huge 1978

single success, but what's the name of the tie-in album?

9. Who, in 1978, is *Jesus Of Cool*?

10. The 1978 television special *All You Need Is Cash* celebrates which fictional pop group?

11. Who is the production brains behind the Village People?

12. Kraftwerk's 1978 long-playing offering comes in a distinctive red-and-black Modernist-style sleeve. What is the title?

13. Although it benefits from additional studio tweaking, *Live And Dangerous* becomes an instant classic rock live album. Which band takes the plaudits?

14. The Cars make their first impact in Britain late in 1978 with which Top 3 single?

15. Which bunch of edgy US new wavers has a minor hit with a version of Al Green's 'Take Me To The River'?

THE OGWT YEARS
1979

1. After Ozzy Osbourne is booted out of Black Sabbath, he is replaced by which ex-Rainbow frontman?

2. 'Rapper's Delight' is a pioneering hip hop record for a group whose name was adapted from their label, all the brainchild of ex-Pillow Talk hitmaker Sylvia Robinson. Who are they?

3. A one-time associate of Sex Pistols' manager Malcolm McLaren, Robin Scott enjoys a moment of fame thanks to the unashamedly infectious Number 2 hit single 'Pop Muzik'. To which group name is the song credited?

4. The Who return to live appearances for the first time since the death of Keith Moon in 1978. Who fills the drum stool?

5. Among the acts brought in to flesh out the Sex Pistols' film *The Great Rock'n'Roll Swindle* is a potential Johnny Rotten replacement who gurns his way through a song called 'Who Killed Bambi'? Who is he?

6. Which one-time progressive rock band hits a commercial peak with the *Breakfast In America* album?

7. Chuck E.'s 'In Love' was the only British hit single for which US singer?

8. The Stranglers' iconic bassist Jean-Jacques Burnel breaks out with a Top 40 solo album. What's it called?

9. When mainman Lowell George quits the group, then promptly dies of a heart attack, Little Feat return to the studio to finish off their final album. What is its title?

10. 1979 sees Keith Richards and Ronnie Wood take an all-star band on the road under which name?

11. Who are the *Three Imaginary Boys*?

12. Which band appear on the cover of their debut album topless and covered in mud?

13. Which punk-pop anthem makers sing the praises of the 'Hersham Boys'?

14. The 1970s have witnessed extraordinary musical changes but, as the decade comes to a close, Status Quo can still be relied upon to bring boogie rock back into the British Top 10. Which single is it this time?

15. Sister Sledge enjoy two British Top 10 singles during 1979, 'We Are Family' and which similarly infectious predecessor?

THE OGWT YEARS
1980

1. Which reclusive musician spends part of the summer in Bermuda before returning home to New York to begin work on what will be his final album?

2. Which lo-fi trio are *Colossal Youth*?

3. *Wheels Of Steel* is Saxon's highest-charting British album. But who's the band's lead singer?

4. *Empty Glass* is the first solo album proper for which guitarist and elder statesman of rock?

5. Talk of the emergence of neo-psychedelia receives a boost with the release of the debut Echo And The Bunnymen album. What is it called?

6. Who are *Searching For The Young Soul Rebels*?

7. Despite the sudden departure of their drummer and guitarist, which band pulls it together to record their third album, *Kaleidoscope*?

8. Which bass-playing frontman is *Solo In Soho*?

9. Who poses the Top 10 question 'Do You Feel My Love'?

10. Which African drumbeat do Adam And The Ants incorporate into their new, post-punk sound?

11. Which ABBA singer handles the poignant lead vocal on 'The Winner Takes It All'?

12. Blondie's hit 'The Tide Is High' is written by which reggae artist?

13. Indie trio Young Marble Giants release their one and only album. What's it called?

14. The Vapors' 'Turning Japanese' is about a) travel b) a card game c) masturbation

15. Grace Jones's *Warm Leatherette* is recorded in which high-tech studio in the Bahamas?

THE OGWT YEARS
1981

1. Billy Idol quits which band to embark on a US-orientated solo career?

2. Which Motown artist enjoys a solo renaissance with the 'Being With You' hit single and album?

3. Hanoi Rocks make their album debut with *Bangkok Shocks, Saigon Shakes, Hanoi Rocks*. But which country do the band call home?

4. Brian Eno and David Byrne unite for which pioneering album of sampled sound and world music?

5. Which music industry legend is, according to his 1981 album, *The Dude*?

6. What, in physical terms, is unusual about The Fall's *Slates*?

7. Which hugely successful British film, directed by Hugh Hudson, is scored by Vangelis?

8. Who is the singer of *Beyond The Valley Of 1984* band The Plasmatics?

9. What, besides a half-full glass of water, lies on the table as depicted on the cover of Yoko Ono's *Season Of Glass* album?

10. Who is the rock 'n' rollin' father of 'Kids In America' hitmaker Kim Wilde?

11. What is the 1981 follow-up to Marianne Faithfull's *Broken English* comeback album?

12. Michael Jackson's hit 'One Day In Your Life' first appeared on an earlier solo album. Which one?

13. Dave Stewart and Barbara Gaskin's chart-topping cover of 'It's My Party' was previously a 1963 hit for which US singer?

14. Meat Loaf's 'Dead Ringer For Love', taken from his 1981 *Dead Ringer* album, is a collaboration with which actress/singer?

15. Which rock veteran makes a surprise appearance in the British singles chart with '(Si Si) Je Suis Un Rock Star'?

THE OGWT YEARS
1982

1. Which historic US site does Ozzy Osbourne famously utilise as a public toilet?

2. The B-52's mini-album *Mesapotamia* is produced by which new wave luminary?

3. *Death Wish II*, directed by Michael Winner, is scored by his rock star guitarist neighbour. Who is he?

4. Lou Reed's 1982 album *The Blue Mask* finds him linking up with a fellow guitarist whose enthusiasm for the Velvet Underground in the late 1960s prompted him to record gigs – later to be issued with the group's blessing. Who is he?

5. *The Gift*, the final Jam studio album, includes the band's penultimate Number 1 single. What is it?

6. Which member of The Clash sings 'Should I Stay Or Should I Go'?

7. Which Rolling Stones live album begins with a snatch of Duke Ellington music?

8. Whose 'The Hunter Gets Captured By The Game' is covered on Blondie's 1982 album, *The Hunter*?

9. Survivor's 'Eye Of The Tiger' is the theme to which Rocky film?

10. Luther Vandross co-writes several songs for and produces which Aretha Franklin album?

11. Which country does Killing Joke's frontman Jaz Coleman disappear to?

12. Which electronic soloist declares himself *I, Assassin*?

13. Celebrated photographer Anton Corbijn takes the cover shot for what turns out to be Captain Beefheart's last album. What's it called?

14. Joe Cocker and Jennifer Warnes sing 'Up Where We Belong', the lead song in *An Officer and a Gentleman*. Which future husband and wife, together with lyricist Will Jennings, are the songwriters?

15. David Bowie collaborates with Giorgio Moroder on which 1982 single?

THE OGWT YEARS
1983

1. Which U2 album becomes the band's first British Number 1?

2. Which star of Woodstock is sentenced to five years' jail on drug charges?

3. For three days late in the year, Nick Cave, Marc Almond and Lydia Lunch gig under which umbrella name?

4. Who co-produces and co-writes several songs on Malcolm McLaren's *Duck Rock* album?

5. Which metal act takes Slade's 'Cum On Feel The Noize' into the US Top 5?

6. Which future 1990s Britpop faves debut with the low-key album release *It*?

7. What is the title of Metallica's debut album?

8. Neil Young is assisted by the Shocking Pinks for which rockabilly-flavoured album?

9. Which acclaimed video production team directs the promo video for Herbie Hancock's hit single *Rockit*?

10. John Lydon again flouts convention by delivering a set of near lounge-style versions of PiL songs on which live album?

11. Which emerging artist hides behind the alias The The?

12. Who provides the guitar break on Michael Jackson's 'Beat It'?

13. Where in London is Electric Avenue, eulogised on Eddy Grant's hit single?

14. Which founder member of ZTT is the label's chief ideologue, responsible for the label's influential slogans and campaign strategies?

15. Who is the model in the video for Billy Joel's Uptown Girl'? (And, reader, she married him!)

THE OGWT YEARS
1984

1.   What soft drinks brand commercial is Michael Jackson filming when he burns his scalp?

2.   Nick Cave And The Bad Seeds launch their career with a version of which 1969 Elvis Presley hit?

3.   Elton John marries. Who's the bride?

4.   Whose hits-packed breakthrough album *She's So Unusual* enters the British album chart?

5.   What is the title of the fictional album in the 1984 spoof film *This Is Spinal Tap*?

6.   Whose breakthrough single is 'Your Love Is King'?

7.   Which continental singer tops the British singles chart with a song titled '99 Luftballons' in her own language?

8.   Which British pop act make an unprecedented appearance in China?

9.   Extraordinarily, a member of Fleetwood Mac files for bankruptcy. Who is he?

10. Who returns to the Top 30 singles chart for the first time in 15 years with a cover of a recent indie hit – backed by the original artists?

11. A US politician's wife is the prime mover behind the Parents Music Resource Center, which is dedicated to censoring overt references to sex and violence in contemporary music. Who is she?

12. Television hippie 'Neil', a character from *The Young Ones*, returns which psychedelic pop single back to the Number 2 position it occupied 17 years earlier?

13. From where in the British Isles do The Alarm hail?

14. Both Roger Waters and David Gilmour release solo albums this year. What does David call his?

15. After a long career, which US vocal trio score their biggest hit single with 'Automatic'?

THE OGWT YEARS
1985

1. Who in 1985 replaces David Lee Roth as Van Halen vocalist?

2. What is the name of Madonna's first tour?

3. Which music industry legend outbids Paul McCartney for the publishing rights to much of the Beatles' song catalogue?

4. Dee Snider is the frontman of which band, though he will quit in 1987?

5. Guitarist D. Boon's death in December 1985 brings the career of which US hardcore band to a premature end?

6. Which hip hop trio adopt a more guitar-friendly sound for their 1985 album, *King Of Rock*?

7. 1985 sees the release of a collection of previously unreleased Velvet Underground outtakes. What is it called?

8. *Behind The Sun* is a 1985 solo album by which rock guitar legend?

9. Sonic Youth invoke an old Creedence Clearwater Revival song for the title of their 'coming out' album. What is it?

10. Which one-time progressive rock frontman

provides the soundtrack for the mid-1980s Alan Parker-directed film *Birdy*?

11. Duranies Andy and John Taylor recruit which singer for their short-lived project the Power Station?

12. Who styles himself *Mr Bad Guy*?

13. Eurythmics collaborate with which soul legend for 'Sisters Are Doin' It For Themselves'?

14. Which 1985 Dire Straits album is credited with giving the new CD format a boost?

15. Larry Blackmon is better known as the mainstay of which long-running New York funk group?

THE OGWT YEARS
1986

1. A collection of John Lennon outtakes from 1973 and 1974 is titled after a road he lived in during his childhood. What was it?

2. Whose band's *Licensed To Ill* debut album took hip hop to the rock masses?

3. Which group suggest that we 'Walk Like An Egyptian'?

4. Robert Palmer's hit 'Addicted To Love' was originally intended to be a duet with a) Whitney Houston b) Gloria Estefan c) Chaka Khan?

5. The Rock And Roll Hall of Fame begins its annual roll of honour. But in which city is the museum based?

6. A Bruce Springsteen box set, *Live 1975/85*, is spread across how many vinyl discs?

7. Slayer go global with *Reign In Blood*, their first album via which influential label?

8. 'Harlem Shuffle', covered by the Stones, was previously a hit for which 1960s soul duo?

9. 'The Final Countdown' hitmakers Europe come from which European country?

10. Who was 'Mike' in Mike + The Mechanics?

11. The Damned are dropped by their record label after their 1986 album. What is it called?

12. Kate Bush re-records which song for her 1986 compilation album, *The Whole Story*?

13. What is the score, according to the Housemartins?

14. Alice Cooper is back posing with snakes again – for which album?

15. 'Eric B. Is President' is the explosive debut single by which Queens-based hip hop duo?

THE OGWT YEARS
1987

1. Which power ballad specialists sing meaningfully about the 'China In Your Hand'?

2. Kim Wilde revives which 1966 Supremes classic?

3. k.d. lang still has a backing band in 1987. They're called the Reclines. She also has a British rock 'n' roll producer who brings the best out of her second album, *Angel With A Lariat*. Who is he?

4. Which hugely influential hip hop collective debut with the *Yo! Bum Rush The Show* album?

5. Even their album titles are making the Grateful Dead sound old!

6. In a nod to the Beatles, U2 shoot the video for which single on a rooftop?

7. Who are the dynamic 'Push It' duo?

8. Tiffany's 'I Think We're Alone Now' was previously a hit for the late 1960s 'Mony Mony' hitmakers. Who were they?

9. *Rhyme Pays* is the debut album by which future hip hop elder statesman?

10. This year's Pink Floyd reunion album started life as a David Gilmour solo effort. He was

obviously having… (insert title)?

11. *Scum* is the debut album by a British hardcore band that is taking thrash to thrilling new extremes. Who are these noisy blighters?

12. Marianne Faithfull revisits her debut single in significantly smokier fashion on her *Strange Weather* album. The title's still the same, though.

13. Guns N' Roses explode into the collective rock consciousness with their debut album. Title?

14. Def Leppard's follow-up to *Pyromania* is enormous, topping the charts on both sides of the Atlantic. What's it called?

15. 1987 sees perhaps the most controversial of all David Bowie tours – in that it is not universally praised. What does he call this highly theatrical venture?

SIDE B

ABBA

Many insist it's possible to measure the 1970s in terms of ABBA songs. OK, now you try matching the song and the year...

1. 'Chiquitita'

2. 'The Winner Takes It All'

3. 'Summer Night City'

4. 'The Name Of The Game'

5. 'Mamma Mia'

6. 'Waterloo'

7. 'Super Trouper'

8. 'One Of Us'

9. 'Does Your Mother Know'

10. 'Fernando'

11. 'Knowing Me, Knowing You'

12. 'Take A Chance On Me'

13. 'SOS'

14. 'Money, Money, Money'

15. 'Dancing Queen'

AC/DC

1. Who is Angus Young's elder brother and fellow AC/DC guitarist?

2. What was the first AC/DC single to chart in Britain?

3. The Young brothers' elder sibling George was once a member of which 1960s Australian pop band?

4. Brian Johnson's former band Geordie had their biggest hit in 1973. What was it?

5. The 1976 worldwide release of *High Voltage* was a compilation made up of material from the original 1975 *High Voltage* album plus a second Australian-only title. What was it?

6. In which British city was the 1978 live album *If You Want Blood You've Got It* recorded?

7. In which popular North London music venue did Bon Scott spend his last night?

8. How many times does the bell toll at the start of 'Hells Bells' on the *Back In Black* album before the band can be heard?

9. What was the first AC/DC album to top the US charts?

10. When the band produced their own album, this 1983 set met with a more lukewarm response. What was it?

11. 1986's *Who Made Who* album was the soundtrack to which film directed by novelist Stephen King?

12. The Young brothers grew up in Australia, but in which country were they born?

13. With which make of guitar is Angus Young best associated?

14. Prior to working with AC/DC for 1979's *Highway To Hell*, producer Mutt Lange produced which Number 1 single for new wavers Boomtown Rats?

15. Bon Scott's distinctive, high octane vocals were inspired by his 1950s rock 'n' roll hero. Who was he?

ALICE COOPER

1. Which actress/singer charted with a cover of Alice Cooper's 'Only Women Bleed' in winter 1977/1978?

2. Drummer Neal Smith's pet snake starred on the cover of Alice Cooper's 1971 album, *Killer*. But was its name a) Karina b) Katrina c) Kachina?

3. Which thrash metal band covered 'I'm Eighteen' in 1984?

4. Which Alice Cooper album came wrapped in a pair of girls' knickers?

5. A variant of the 1972 hit 'Elected' appeared on the band's 1969 debut album *Pretties For You* under what slightly different title?

6. Alice Cooper's father was a) a preacher b) a lawyer c) an owner of a wax museum?

7. The band found fame after moving from Los Angeles to which midwest city?

8. Which producer teamed up with the band for *Love It To Death* and helped usher in their trademark sound?

9. *Killer* is which punk star's favourite album?

10. Which track on the *School's Out* album worked in elements from *West Side Story*?

11. Megadeth covered 'No More Mr Nice Guy' in

which 1989 Wes Craven film?

12. Which British folk rock singer duetted with Alice on the 'Billion Dollar Babies' title track?

13. Cooper revived his career in 1989 with the hit single 'Poison'. From which album did it come?

14. Instrumental in creating the band's early costumes was the sister of the band's drummer Neal Smith, Cindy. Which member of the group did she marry?

15. In 1976, Cooper, now solo, released a concert film. What was it called?

BAD COMPANY / FREE

1. Bad Company frontman was ex-Free frontman Paul Rodgers. Who was the guitarist?

2. What was the name of guitarist Paul Kossoff's post-Free band?

3. Bad Company bassist Boz Burrell previously played with which progressive rock outfit?

4. Bad Company were signed to which band's Swan Song label?

5. 'Young Blood', a US Top 20 single in 1976, was originally a hit for which 1950s vocal group?

6. Paul Rodgers and Jimmy Page teamed up in the 1980s for two albums under which band name?

7. After Free collapsed in 1973, bassist Andy Fraser formed which band?

8. Bassist Tetsu Yamauchi played on which Free album?

9. Who produced *Tons Of Sobs*?

10. Free guitarist Paul Kossoff was the son of which British actor?

11. Paul Kossoff's post-Free band took its name from his solo album released in which year?

12. The surprise break-up of Free in spring 1971, prompted the autumn release of which album?

13. In 2011, it was revealed that Paul Rodgers was once in line to join a revived version of which legendary late-1960s Californian-based rock band?

14. Which Bad Company album featured a pair of dice on the cover?

15. When Mick Ralphs and Simon Kirke reformed Bad Company in 1986, who did they enlist as singer?

THE BAND

1. What was the Band's highest-charting British hit single?

2. The Band scored a British Top 20 hit in 1970 with 'Rag Mama Rag'. The following year, who went several places better with a version of 'The Night They Drove Old Dixie Down'?

3. In 1973, after a quartet of era-defining studio albums, The Band switched from Americana to 1950s rock 'n' roll nostalgia with which album?

4. In 1976, The Band released a cover version of which Ray Charles song in support of Jimmy Carter's bid for the US presidency?

5. The Band started life as Ronnie Hawkins' backing band, The Hawks. But which future R&B standard did Hawkins' cousin Dale write and release in 1957?

6. Years before directing *The Last Waltz*, Martin Scorsese cut his teeth working on which festival film?

7. A re-recording of 'This Wheel's On Fire' was later used as the theme to the BBC comedy series, *Absolutely Fabulous*. Who was the singer?

8. Which Band song was used on the *Easy Rider* soundtrack?

9. Which US drummer replaced Levon Helm when

The Band accompanied Bob Dylan on his 1966 world tour?

10. In which New York State hamlet is the Big Pink house located?

11. Which song on Robbie Robertson's 1987 self-titled solo album featured a guest vocal from U2's Bono?

12. Which Band member played Loretta Lynn's father in the 1980 film *Coal Miner's Daughter*?

13. Which virtuoso guitarist, on hearing *Music From Big Pink*, declared that it had changed his life, quit his band and changed musical direction?

14. Which one of the following artists was not in *The Last Waltz*? a) Neil Diamond b) Joni Mitchell c) David Crosby

15. *The Basement Tapes*, recorded during 1967 with Bob Dylan, eventually surfaced officially on record in which year?

THE BEACH BOYS

1. The Beach Boys released a song by cult hippie leader Charles Manson on the B-side of their 1968 single 'Bluebirds Over The Mountain'. Originally called 'Cease To Exist', the band gave it an equally mystifying title. What was it?

2. Brian Wilson publicly debuted his 'Surf's Up' song on a 1967 US television special hosted by who?

3. 'I'm So Young' is one of several classics on the Beach Boys' 1965 album *Today!* But which doo wop vocal group released the 1958 original?

4. What was the name of the Beach Boys' home studio?

5. Only one of the Beach Boys materialised alongside The Beatles in the Maharishi's Rishikesh hideaway in the foothills of the Himalayas. Who was he?

6. Who handles lead vocal, alongside Brian Wilson, on the Beach Boys' version of the old Regents hit 'Barbara Ann'?

7. In 1968, the Beach Boys released an album of instrumental versions of many of their best-known songs. The title?

8. The Beach Boys hail from which small-sized city in Los Angeles County?

9. In 1979, the Beach Boys remade one of their late 1960s songs as an 11-minute disco workout. Which was the unfortunate composition?

10. What make of car was a 409?

11. Carnie and Wendy, Brian Wilson's two daughters from his first marriage, teamed up with another celebrity scion for Wilson Phillips. Who was she – and watch that spelling!

12. Soon after producing three-piece girl group The Honeys, Brian Wilson married one of them. Who was she?

13. Who was the controversial therapist who began treating Brian Wilson in the mid 1970s, going on to manage him for much of the following decade?

14. The mantra-like 'Transcendental Meditation' appeared on which Beach Boys album?

15. A Bruce Johnson song became a Grammy-winning mid-1970s hit for Barry Manilow. What was it?

THE BEATLES

1. Which Beatles hit was recorded by The Damned for the B-side of their 1976 single 'New Rose'?

2. Which popular US hard rock band made an unlikely appearance in the *Sgt Pepper's Lonely Hearts Club Band* film performing The Beatles' 'Come Together'?

3. Paul McCrawfish, John McCrawfish, George McCrawfish and Ringo Starfish were pseudonyms used on a 1974 album by which San Franciscan experimental band?

4. Who played drums on the 1962 single 'Love Me Do'?

5. In what year did The Beatles make their record-breaking appearance at Shea Stadium in New York?

6. To which British journalist did John Lennon first insist that the Beatles were 'more popular than Jesus'?

7. What was the last song recorded by The Beatles (though John Lennon was absent) before their split was announced in April 1970?

8. What was the original title for the *Let It Be* album?

9. Which one of these *Let It Be* songs was not recorded at the January 1969 rooftop concert?

a) 'One After 909' b) 'Dig It' c) 'I've Got A Feeling'

10. Which 'White Album' song, written by John Lennon, was a thinly disguised attack on the Maharishi?

11. The Beatles resisted releasing 'Ob-La-Di, Ob-La-Da' on single in Britain in 1968. But which Scottish band took it to the top of the charts?

12. What year saw the release of those two famous 'Red' and 'Blue' Beatles double-album compilations?

13. In which year did the Beatles receive MBEs?

14. Who was the second-oldest Beatle?

15. 'Yesterday' was the first Beatles song to feature just one Beatle. What was the second?

BEE GEES

1. What was the title of Bee Gee Robin Gibb's first solo single?

2. Barbra Streisand received the Bee Gees' treatment for her 1980 album *Guilty*. Which brother did most of the writing and producing?

3. The Bee Gees' flop television show from 1970 was matched by a similarly titled flop album. What was it called?

4. When advance copies of the Bee Gees' spring 1967 single were sent out to radio stations, the buzz was that this supposedly new group from Australia were in fact The Beatles. What was the record?

5. Which Gibb brothers song, a British flop for the band in 1967, quickly became a standard with Janis Joplin and Nina Simone among those first to cover it.

6. How many consecutive non-charting British albums did the Bee Gees endure during the 1970s before the enormous success of *Saturday Night Fever* in 1977? a) 3 b) 5 c) 7

7. Robin Gibb's solo career got off to a successful start with the Top 3 hit single 'Saved By The Bell', but his debut album flopped. What was it called?

8. The Bee Gees' first US Number 1 single went

nowhere in Britain, which is all the more surprising because it's since become a standard. What was it?

9. The Gibb brothers wrote Diana Ross's first British Number 1 hit single since 1971's 'I'm Still Waiting'. What was it?

10. Younger brother Andy Gibb's last single of note was a version of the Everly Brothers' 'All I Have To Dream', a duet with his then girlfriend. Who was she?

11. Maurice Gibb married his first wife Lulu in February 1969. Several weeks later, she was representing the UK in the Eurovision Song Contest with which song?

12. The Bee Gees wrote and recorded 'More Than A Woman' for the *Saturday Night Fever* soundtrack, but which act had the hit with it?

13. The Bee Gees starred alongside which recently hugely successful artist in a 1978 film adaptation of The Beatles' *Sgt Pepper's Lonely Hearts Club Band*?

14. Who is the Australian-born impresario whose influence guided the Bee Gees to many of their biggest successes?

15. Which critically acclaimed late 1960s Bee Gees album came in an expensively produced flocked red cover with gold lettering?

CHUCK BERRY

1. Chuck Berry's 60th birthday concert was celebrated with a tie-in film and soundtrack. But which of Chuck's numerous champions acted as the event's Musical Director?

2. Chuck is a nickname for Berry's birth name... which is?

3. Chuck's first British Top 10 album was *Chuck Berry On Stage*. In which year did it chart?

4. When did Chuck release his last studio album? a) 1971 b) 1979 c) 1999

5. What on-stage dance move is Chuck Berry known for?

6. 1972's 'My Ding-a-Ling' gave Chuck Berry the biggest hit of his career. On which album did it appear soon after in unedited form?

7. On his 1967 concert album, *Live At The Fillmore Auditorium*, Berry is backed by members of which aspiring San Francisco psychedelic blues rock band?

8. Berry extemporised on 'Johnny B Goode' with a side-long title track on which 1969 album?

9. Which Berry classic received an orchestral rock makeover from ELO in 1973?

10. 'Joe Joe Gun' was a little-known 1958 Chuck

Berry single. But from which group did early 1970s boogie rockers Jo Jo Gunne emerge?

11. In December 1978, Keith Richards released a version of which vintage Berry number as a Christmas 45?

12. Who was Berry's long-serving pianist, some-time arranger and the man responsible for a 1991 solo album, *Johnnie B. Bad*?

13. Jimi Hendrix had a posthumous mini-hit in Britain in 1972 with a version of 'Johnny B. Goode' recorded – and filmed – at which legendary concert?

14. The Beach Boys based their 1963 hit 'Surfin' USA' on which Chuck Berry song?

15. John Lennon and Yoko Ono invited Chuck Berry to duet with them on whose US talk show in 1972?

BLACK SABBATH

1. When Ozzy Osbourne was fired from the band in spring 1979, who replaced him?

2. Black Sabbath formed in 1968 as a) Earth b) Wind c) Fire

3. What song on the band's debut album begins with short passage of Geezer Butler playing bass through a wah-wah pedal?

4. Tony Iommi can be seen in the Rolling Stones' 1968 shot-for-TV spectacular, *Rock 'n' Roll Circus*, playing guitar with which group?

5. Who was the legendary horror film star of the 1963 film *Black Sabbath*?

6. Who was the producer of the first three Sabbath albums?

7. Which Sabbath single managed a Top 30 chart placing in 1978?

8. Sharon Osbourne's father was a music biz heavyweight who managed the Small Faces and ELO as well as Black Sabbath. Who was he?

9. Sabbath toured the States in 1980 as part of a co-headlining tour known as *Black And Blue*. Which band was 'blue'?

10. What is Black Sabbath's only Number 1 chart album?

11. In the mid-1980s Tony Iommi was engaged to which ex-member of the Runaways?

12. Which of Ozzy and Sharon Osbourne's three children did not participate in the MTV reality show *The Osbournes*? a) Jack b) Kelly c) Aimee

13. What is Ozzy's birth name?

14. Who was the guitarist in Osbourne's band who died in a light aircraft tragedy in March 1982?

15. Ozzy Osbourne played up the satanic reputation in 1980 with 'Mr Crowley', a single lifted from which solo album?

BLONDIE
/ DEBBIE HARRY

1. The first Blondie releases appeared on which short-lived New York-based record label?

2. Between her time with a late 1960s harmony group and Blondie, Debbie Harry starred in which early 1970s New York City girl group covers band?

3. Who was the hyperactive bassist turned writer who rivalled Debbie Harry in the visual cool stakes during Blondie's pre-fame times?

4. In spring 1978, 'Denis' shot to Number a) 1 b) 2 c) 3 in the British singles chart?

5. On which album sleeve did Debbie Harry's face appear airbrushed and pierced by art director HR Giger?

6. What's the connection between David Soul's 1976 hit 'Don't Give Up On Us' and Blondie?

7. Which Debbie Harry album was the last to feature Andy Warhol artwork before the artist's death in 1987?

8. A decade prior to Blondie's initial success, Debbie Harry made her album debut with which folk-rock act?

9. After Gary Valentine's departure in 1977,

Blondie enjoyed a huge hit with which one of his songs?

10. What's the name of the band's drummer with the 1960s mod haircut?

11. Blondie's first international success, 'Denis', was originally a 1963 hit (as 'Denise') for which New York vocal group?

12. Which well-known Blondie song was initially known within the band as 'The Disco Song'?

13. Ex-King Crimson guitarist Robert Fripp guested on which *Parallel Lines* album track?

14. Which Blondie single made a notable appearance in a 1980 crime drama starring Richard Gere?

15. Debbie Harry's 1981 solo album *KooKoo* was a collaboration with which hot production team?

MARC BOLAN
AND T. REX

1. One unlikely legacy of Bolan's short-lived spell with 1960s pop-art combo John's Children was a single, withdrawn at the time of its release in summer 1967, that's now one of the most valuable on the collector's market. Title?

2. Bolan once famously said he was a star, even at the age of eight, on the streets of what district of inner-city London?

3. Bolan's bongo-playing Tyrannosaurus Rex sidekick Steve Peregrine Took was plain Steven Porter from London before his partner renamed him, taking inspiration from which classic fantasy book?

4. In spring 1970, Bolan and producer Tony Visconti recorded a bubblegum-inspired 45 under which fictional name?

5. Before restyling himself 'the Electric Warrior' in 1971, Bolan claimed to have been given a few electric guitar lessons from which leading British blues-rock player?

6. The only time glam gurus Bolan and Bowie recorded together in a studio was in January 1970 for Bowie's flop follow-up to 'Space Oddity'. The title?

7. Bolan's early hit singles featured backing vocals from US duo Flo and Eddie, better known as Mark Volman and Howard Kaylan from which successful 1960s singing group?

8. Which noted 1970s keyboard player guested on T. Rex's third successive hit 45, 'Get It On'?

9. Ringo Starr directed the 1972 Bolan feature film *Born To Boogie*, but which children's TV actor made a notable appearance during the Mad Hatter's Tea-Party scene?

10. Which 1960s singing star, then hosting her own television show, duetted with Bolan in 1973 on his song 'Life's A Gas'?

11. The Power Station, featuring Robert Palmer on vocals, enjoyed a transatlantic hit with which T. Rex song in 1985?

12. Which radio DJ recited poems on two Tyrannosaurus Rex albums?

13. Bolan's post-glam *Zinc Alloy* album, released in 1974, doubled as an alter-ego. But who were his fictional backing band?

14. In 1976, Bolan and his partner Gloria Jones duetted on a version of which classic Phil Spector hit?

15. Bolan made his last public appearance jamming on stage alongside an old mate at the end of a six-part television series, *Marc*. Who was he?

DAVID BOWIE

1. Bowie shares a birthday with another legendary rock performer. Who?

2. The bulk of 1975's *Young Americans* album was taped at the studio home of Gamble & Huff's fashionable 'Philadelphia Sound'. What was it called?

3. A member of beat-era combo The Kon-Rads during 1963, Bowie was neither the band's guitarist nor its sole vocalist. What was his main instrument?

4. On what album sleeve did Bowie appear wearing what he later called 'a man's dress'?

5. Mick Ronson, the guitarist Bowie called 'my Jeff Beck', had previously been a member of which Hull-based band?

6. Who was the model pictured alongside Bowie on the sleeve of his 1973 album of cover versions, *Pin-Ups*?

7. In October 1973, Bowie filmed a TV special at London's Marquee Club. Its title?

8. What was the full name of the character Bowie played in Nic Roeg's 1976 film, *The Man Who Fell To Earth*?

9. What was Bowie's first British Number 1 single?

10. Bowie's 1977 hit single 'Sound And Vision' featured which husband and wife team on backing vocals?

11. A second 1977 hit 45, '"Heroes"', was inspired by the Berlin Wall a short distance away from where the song was recorded. What was the name of the studio?

12. In 1980, Bowie played the title role in *The Elephant Man* on the Broadway stage. What was the character's real name?

13. In 1974, Bowie had a Top 10 hit with a live version of whose 'Knock On Wood'?

14. What was the title of Bowie's 1997 'drum and bass' album?

15. Who was the 'Rock Dreams' man, whose 'dog's bollocks' portrayal of David Bowie for the cover of 1974's *Diamond Dogs* prompted a modesty preserving swipe of the record company airbrush.

JAMES BROWN

1. What is the title of James Brown's 1963 live album, widely considered to be among the best ever concert performances?

2. In 1981, funky post-punk act Pigbag took an old James Brown song title and had punning fun with it. What was the name of their hit?

3. During the 1960s and 1970s, James Brown only had one British Top 20 hit single, and that was in 1966. Which classic was that?

4. What black consciousness anthem did Brown unleash on the States in summer 1968 after the spring assassination of Dr Martin Luther King?

5. The Rolling Stones had the dubious honour of following Brown's astonishing performance at a legendary October 1964 concert, filmed and released under what title?

6. James Brown's 'Funky Drummer' 45 includes one of the most sampled drum breaks ever. But when was the single first released?

7. Who was the legendary bassist with Brown's early 1970s backing band the J.B.'s?

8. What is the full title of Brown's classic 1970 single 'Sex Machine'?

9. In lending his support to which US presidential candidate, Brown temporarily damaged his

reputation among the black community.

10. Which 1967 single is generally regarded as Brown's watershed release, after which he was always associated with the funk genre?

11. Who was Muhammad Ali's opponent in Zaire in 1974 at the famous 'Rumble In The Jungle' fight where Brown performed at a huge pre-fight music festival?

12. James Brown – and his song 'Living In America' – appeared in which *Rocky* film?

13. What was the name of Brown's back-up band of vocalists and dancers, who stayed with him from the mid 1950s until the late 1960s?

14. James Brown died on Christmas Day. But in what year?

15. Which musician provided the link between James Brown and 'Fame'-era David Bowie?

KATE BUSH

1. What was Kate Bush's first self-produced album?

2. During 1977, Bush played the pub circuit in and around London fronting her own band. What was the name?

3. Which Elton John song was given a reggae-style makeover by Bush in 1991?

4. Which member of Pink Floyd co-produced Bush's 1978 debut album, *The Kick Inside*?

5. The album version of the 1985 hit 'Running Up That Hill' has a subtitle. What is it?

6. Which Kate Bush album was recorded on the French Riviera?

7. What is the name of Kate's older brother, who has worked with her since she was a young teenager?

8. What was Bush's first Number 1 album?

9. Bush has sung vocals on three Peter Gabriel hits, including 'Games Without Frontiers' and 'Don't Give Up'. What was the third, released in 1980?

10. Bush wrote a tribute to which English classical composer on her 1980 album, *Never For Ever*?

11. In what year did Kate Bush hope 'December Will Be Magic Again'?

12. Kate Bush made a rare live appearance in March 1987 where, joined by David Gilmour, she graced *The Secret Policeman's Third Ball*. What song did the pair perform?

13. In spring 1979, Bush did something that – to date – she's not repeated during her career. What?

14. The 1993 album *The Red Shoes* was inspired by a 1948 British film classic directed by Michael Powell and Emeric Pressburger. Who played the film's lead?

15. Which Beatles song did Bush perform live during her 'pub rock' period? a) 'Come Together' b) 'Dear Prudence' c) 'The Fool On The Hill'

ERIC CLAPTON

1. After the much-loved *Layla And Other Assorted Love Songs* double album, Derek And The Dominos followed up with a lesser-known live album. Title?

2. Eric Clapton made a one-off tour of which country with George Harrison in 1991?

3. Clapton's coming-of-age vocal performance was on a 1969 Cream single. What was it?

4. Who was bassist in Derek And The Dominos and a regular Clapton sideman for years afterwards?

5. Which fellow guitarist was the motivating force behind Clapton's comeback show at the Rainbow Theatre, London, in 1973?

6. Clapton's self-titled debut solo album from 1970 included the first of several JJ Cale cover versions he's recorded down the years. What was it?

7. The muted treble guitar sound Clapton was famous for in the late 1960s was known by what name?

8. What was an album track on Clapton's 1977 album, *Slowhand*, a 1991 live single, and was inspired by wife-to-be, Patti Boyd?

9. The short-lived 1969 Blind Faith supergroup consisted of Clapton, Steve Winwood, Ginger

Baker and a bass player recruited from Family. Who?

10. What was the name of the impromptu supergroup that featured Clapton alongside John Lennon, Keith Richards, Mitch Mitchell and Yoko Ono for a one-off appearance at the Rolling Stones' *Rock 'n' Roll Circus*?

11. What role did Clapton play in the 1975 Ken Russell film version of *Tommy*? a) The Pinball Wizard b) The Preacher c) Himself

12. On which album sleeve is a suited and smoking Clapton standing beside a melted Fender Strat guitar?

13. Which Jimi Hendrix cover was included on the *Layla And Other Assorted Love Songs* album?

14. What was the name Clapton gave to his favourite Fender Stratocaster guitar, a veteran of numerous gigs and studio sessions between 1973 and 1985?

15. At the start of which 1968 album is Clapton heard repeating the words 'Are you hung up?' over a cacophony of sound effects?

THE CLASH

1.   After leaving The Clash in 1983, Mick Jones formed Big Audio Dynamite with which noted reggae DJ?

2.   How was drummer Terry Chimes credited on the sleeve of the first Clash album?

3.   Which traditional song, a 101'ers concert favourite, did The Clash reprise on the *Sandinista* album?

4.   Joe Strummer's pre-Clash outfit The 101'ers also included a drummer who went on to play with PiL and The Raincoats. Who was he?

5.   What was The Clash's first British Top 30 single?

6.   Joe Strummer's father was a) a dishwasher b) a dentist c) a diplomat?

7.   Mick Jones and Joe Strummer were reunited on which Big Audio Dynamite album?

8.   The Slits joined The Clash for the *White Riot* tour in spring 1977. So did the Mortlake-based stalwarts of the previous autumn's 100 Club Punk Rock Festival. Who were they?

9.   The band's debut album version of 'Police And Thieves' became one of the era's best-known punky-reggae cover versions. Who sang the original?

10. 'Guns On The Roof', from The Clash's second album, was inspired by a real-life incident that involved Simonon, Headon and an airgun. What were they shooting at?

11. 'Topper' Headon was the band's drummer in the definitive Clash line-up. But what was his real name?

12. After falling out with original manager Bernie Rhodes, The Clash briefly employed the managerial services of which noted rock writer?

13. The Clash's 1979 *London Calling* album included an old rock 'n' roll cover, 'Brand New Cadillac'. Who recorded the original?

14. 'I Fought The Law', another rock 'n' roll cover, was previously a 1966 hit for who?

15. Since Clash days, bassist Paul Simonon has found gainful employment as a) a painter b) a printer c) a priest?

LEONARD COHEN

1. Long-time Cohen backing singer and collaborator Jennifer Warnes released an album of Cohen covers in 1987. It took its title from which Cohen song?

2. Which Greek island did Cohen make his home for much of the 1960s?

3. *The Favourite Game* is the title of Cohen's first novel, published in 1963. Three years later saw the publication of its better-known follow-up. What was it?

4. Which ex-Velvet Underground member reinterpreted Cohen's 'Hallelujah' for a 1991 Cohen tribute album, setting the template for subsequent cover versions?

5. Who turned Cohen's poem 'God Is Alive, Magic Is Afoot' into an electronically enhanced mantra-song?

6. Nick Cave And The Bad Seeds released a version of Cohen's 'Avalanche' on which 1984 album?

7. What was the collective name of Leonard Cohen's touring band during the early 1970s?

8. Which 1971 Robert Altham film includes several Cohen songs on the soundtrack?

9. Which Cohen release boasted an all-star cast and Phil Spector at the controls?

10. In chart terms, what was Cohen's most successful 1960s album in Britain?

11. Cohen was one of the few old masters to tackle 1980s technology and win, as evidenced on the 1988 album that revived his career. What was it?

12. Cohen's early classic 'Suzanne' was first covered on a 1966 album, *In My Life*. Who was the artist?

13. Which US acid-folk band backed Cohen on a couple of songs on his 1967 debut album, *Songs Of Leonard Cohen*?

14. On which Nirvana song did Kurt Cobain sing of 'a Leonard Cohen afterworld'?

15. Who produced three of Cohen's early and most acclaimed albums and also joined him on tour?

ELVIS COSTELLO

1. Elvis Costello's 1980 hit 'I Can't Stand Up For Falling Down' was a cover of a little-known Stax B-side by which US soul duo?

2. Which Elvis Costello album was originally going to be titled 'Emotional Fascism'?

3. Elvis Costello & the Attractions' 1978 cut '(What's So Funny 'Bout) Peace, Love, And Understanding' was written a few years earlier by which pub rocker?

4. Which mid-1980s Elvis Costello pseudonym subsequently resurfaced years later as a Hollywood film title?

5. Caitlin O'Riordan, who Costello married in 1986, played bass with which distinguished if sometimes ramshackle outfit?

6. With which notable big band did Costello's father, Ross MacManus, sing for many years?

7. Costello's manager suggested that Declan MacManus adopt Elvis Costello as a stage name. Who was he?

8. Costello covered which Bacharach & David song on the *Live Stiffs Live* album?

9. A popular promotional live album, recorded in Canada, circulated during 1978. What was it called?

10. What was by far the biggest of Costello's 1970s singles?

11. On which album cover is Costello seen peering over red-tinted specs?

12. Which author has published at least two novels bearing Costello-inspired titles?

13. In the late 1970s, Costello duetted with his favourite country singer on 'Stranger In The House'. Who is he?

14. Which Costello album featured contributions from various ex-Elvis Presley sidemen?

15. In 1983, Costello released which politically charged 45 under the name 'The Imposter'?

CROSBY, STILLS, NASH AND YOUNG

1. Which member of Crosby, Stills, Nash and Young did not appear on David Crosby's 1971 *If I Could Only Remember My Name* solo set.

2. Graham Nash was reunited with The Hollies in 1983 for the first of two albums. What was it called?

3. Which infamous song about a ménage a trois did David Crosby give to Jefferson Airplane for their 1968 album, *Crown Of Creation*?

4. The Stills-Young Band had a British Top 20 hit in 1976 with which album?

5. Buffalo Springfield's Stephen Stills-penned 'For What It's Worth' was about a) the Kent State shootings b) the assassination of Robert Kennedy c) a curfew on Sunset Strip, Los Angeles

6. Richie Furay and Jim Messina, two of the non-CSN&Y members of Buffalo Springfield, went on to form which country rock act?

7. Crosby, Stills and Nash had their first and only British hit single in 1969. What was it?

8. 'Suite: Judy Blue Eyes' was written about a) Judy Sill b) Judy Collins c) Judy Garland

9. Which member of CSN&Y admitted at the 1969

Woodstock Festival, 'We're scared shitless'?

10. While CSN&Y had the US hit with Joni Mitchell's 'Woodstock', which Fairport Convention spin-off took it to Number 1 in Britain?

11. Which Neil Young song was drawn out for more than 13 minutes on the 1971 live album *4 Way Street*?

12. Which single, lifted from Stephen Stills' 1970 debut solo album, has been covered by Aretha Franklin, Engelbert Humperdinck and Bucks Fizz?

13. Which band did Stills form with ex-Byrds guitarist Chris Hillman in 1971, releasing two albums over the next couple of years?

14. Which was Graham Nash's only British Number 1 single with the Hollies?

15. CSN returned to the US singles chart in 1982 with which Top 10 hit?

MILES DAVIS

1. Who was the innovative Columbia Records producer who worked with Davis from the late 1950s to the early 1980s?

2. Jefferson Airplane's Grace Slick played which Miles Davis album repeatedly while looking for musical inspiration to write the acid-rock classic 'White Rabbit'?

3. She appeared on the cover of Filles de Kilimanjaro, turned Miles Davis on to Jimi Hendrix, and by the mid 1970s, had become a fully fledged, funked-up 'Nasty Girl', the title of her breakthrough record. Who was she?

4. How many British Top 40 albums did Miles Davis notch up? a) 9 b) 4 c) none

5. Who played with various Davis line-ups during the late 1960s before leaving in 1970 to form Return To Forever?

6. With which bebop legend did Miles serve an apprenticeship in the 1940s?

7. Towards the end of his electrifying stint with Davis, which English guitarist broke off in 1970 to release a solo album of spiritually charged material?

8. Which 1972 Davis album, savaged at the time of its release, has since become regarded as milestone in what's now known as avant-funk?

9. 'Mr Pastorius', a tribute to the late bassist Jaco, appeared on which mature-era Davis set?

10. Covers of Cyndi Lauper and Michael Jackson songs appeared on which 1985 Miles Davis album?

11. Davis's 1971 album *A Tribute To Jack Johnson* was a homage to a) a champion heavyweight boxer b) a Civil Rights leader c) his current bass player?

12. Which pianist joined Davis's second great quintet in 1963, was fired in 1968, then made sporadic reappearances at the turn of the decade?

13. Which mid-1980s Miles Davis backing musician ended up playing with the Rolling Stones?

14. In 1985, Davis made an appearance in which popular television show?

15. Davis lent his support to which 1985 protest movement, responsible for the Sun City project?

DEEP PURPLE

1. Which band was playing the Montreux Casino in 1971 when it burnt down, an incident that inspired Deep Purple's 'Smoke On The Water'?

2. In 1975, ex-Deep Purple guitarist Ritchie Blackmore formed Rainbow with the remnants of which New York bar band?

3. Tommy Bolin replaced Ritchie Blackmore as Deep Purple guitarist in 1975. From which band did he jump ship?

4. The carved-in-stone effect of the *In Rock* album sleeve was inspired by which North American landmark?

5. Prior to joining Deep Purple, Ian Gillan and Roger Glover were both members of which club band?

6. Which Deep Purple member was never a part of Whitesnake? a) Jon Lord b) Ian Paice c) Roger Glover?

7. Guitarist Ritchie Blackmore cut his teeth as a session man for which notable early 1960s producer?

8. Who was the band's vocalist on the first three Deep Purple albums?

9. Deep Purple's first taste of singles chart success, at least in the USA, came with a groovy cover of

which Joe South song?

10. Which 1971 Deep Purple hit single has since been regarded as a forerunner of speed metal?

11. Which was the longest song on Purple's 1972 live album, *Made In Japan*?

12. Mid-1970s bass-playing Purple second vocalist Glenn Hughes had previously been part of which early 1970s band?

13. Just weeks after his first appearance on a Deep Purple album, Tommy Bolin's solo debut appeared. What was it called?

14. The classic Deep Purple line-up reunited on which 1984 album?

15. By the end of the 1980s, which member of the reunited band was fired before work began on a third reunion set?

BOB DYLAN

1. What was the first chart-topping Bob Dylan album in Britain?

2. Bob Dylan's appearance, on 15 July 1978, at the Blackbushe aerodrome in Surrey was part of a promotional tour for which album?

3. Who was the documentary maker who followed Dylan during his 1965 tour of Britain for the groundbreaking *Don't Look Back* film?

4. Dylan re-recorded an earlier song, 'Girl From The North Country', with Johnny Cash for which late-1960s album?

5. Which recent Simon and Garfunkel hit did Dylan rework for his 1970 *Self Portrait* album?

6. Dylan acted in and wrote much of the score for the 1973 western *Pat Garrett And Billy The Kid*. Who was the film's director?

7. Who, in 1975, recorded a reggae-flavoured take on Dylan's 'Knockin' On Heaven's Door'?

8. Dylan's son Jakob, born in 1969, later fronted which US rock band?

9. Joan Baez's 1975 album *Diamonds & Rust* featured a cover of which recent Dylan song?

10. Rubin Carter was a boxer whose wrongful conviction for a 1966 murder inspired Dylan to

write which mid-1970s protest song?

11. What album was Dylan recording when he heard the news that Elvis Presley was dead?

12. John Lennon wrote 'Serve Yourself' in response to which late 1970s Dylan song?

13. Which latter-day Dylan classic was left off the 1983 album *Infidels* at the last minute?

14. What was the title of the 1985 career-spanning box set that set the standard for future retrospective rock releases?

15. Which Dylan song did George Harrison cover on the 1970 album *All Things Must Pass*?

THE EAGLES

1.   The Eagles formed after working on which singer's third solo album?

2.   Which quietly established songwriter wrote or co-wrote most of the songs on Don Henley's hugely successful 1984 solo album, *Building The Perfect Beast*?

3.   Glenn Frey co-wrote the band's first hit single with which up and coming country-inclined folkie?

4.   Bernie Leadon had previously lined up with Gram Parsons in which country-rock outfit?

5.   In 1975, The Eagles scored their first US Number 1 hit single. What was it?

6.   Which Eagles album was an homage to the outlaw way of life in the Old West?

7.   Which song on the 1975 *One Of These Nights* album was co-written by Ronald Reagan's daughter Patti, then dating Bernie Leadon?

8.   Having already replaced Randy Meisner in Poco, who stepped in once again to replace him in The Eagles in 1977?

9.   Prior to his stint in The Eagles, Joe Walsh had released three studio albums as part of which rock trio?

10. Which hotel was immortalised on the cover of the *Hotel California* album?

11. Having already appeared on Randy Newman's 1974 set *Good Old Boys*, The Eagles returned in numbers to assist on the 1977 follow-up. What was it called?

12. Which mid-1970s co-write with Jackson Browne was the band's tribute to a 1950s Hollywood legend?

13. Which early Cameron Crowe teen comedy – starring Sean Penn and Jennifer Jason Leigh – featured solo songs from various Eagles members on the soundtrack?

14. Which founder member of The Eagles began his acting career in an episode of *Miami Vice* before securing a role in the 1986 film *Let's Get Harry*?

15. Who sang lead vocal on the track 'Hotel California'?

FLEETWOOD MAC

1. The prototype for the mid-1970s Fleetwood Mac sound can be heard on Lindsay Buckingham and Stevie Nicks' 1973 album. What was the title?

2. How many US Top 10 hit singles came off the back of Fleetwood Mac's 1977 *Rumours* album?

3. Which Mac single was recorded in a baseball stadium and featured a marching band?

4. Who was Peter Green's replacement in John Mayall's Bluesbreakers after he'd quit in 1967 to form Fleetwood Mac?

5. Who was the founder of Mac's first label, Blue Horizon, and producer of their early records?

6. Which 1969 Mac single was split across two sides of the 45?

7. Christine McVie's big hit with Chicken Shack came in 1969 with a cover of a recent Etta James song. What was it?

8. What was the last Fleetwood Mac album to feature guitarist Danny Kirwan?

9. Despite the band's later success, Fleetwood Mac's highest-charting British hit singles date from the blues-rock era, with just one reaching Number 1 early in 1969. What was it?

10. Which US-born Mac member suggested in 1973 that the group relocate to Los Angeles?

11. Which band member wrote two of the four singles lifted from 1977's *Rumours* album?

12. Stevie Nicks' first name is a) Stevie b) Stephanie c) Stovepipe?

13. 'Rhiannon' was based on a folk tale from which country?

14. Fleetwood Mac guitarist Jeremy Spencer famously walked out on the group to join which religious sect?

15. Which band member featured on the cover of the 1968 album *Mr Wonderful*?

ARETHA FRANKLIN

1. Which 1971 Aretha Franklin hit single, a cover
    of a contemporary song that had become an
    instant standard, was prefaced with a nod to the
    Four Tops' 'Still Waters Run Deep'?

2. One of the most distinctive backing singers on
    many classic Aretha Franklin records has been
    her sister. What's her name?

3. Who wrote and first released 'Respect'?

4. Carole King recorded '(You Make Me Feel Like)
    A Natural Woman', a song she'd co-written with
    Jerry Wexler, for her 1971 *Tapestry* album. How
    many years earlier had Aretha enjoyed a US hit
    with the song?

5. Aretha's elder sister sang the original version of
    'Piece Of My Heart'. Who was she?

6. Who hit first with 'I Say A Little Prayer'?

7. What song did Aretha re-record for her
    appearance in the 1980 film *The Blues Brothers*?

8. Which Rolling Stones song did Franklin record
    in the mid 1980s assisted by the band's guitarists
    Keith Richards and Ronnie Wood?

9. Who was the lead singer of the Sweet
    Inspirations, who backed Franklin during her
    late-1960s heyday?

10. Aretha didn't get her first British Number 1 until 1987 – even then it was a duet with George Michael. What was the song called?

11. The 1985 chart hit 'Sisters Are Doin' It For Themselves' was a collaboration with which British synth pop duo?

12. Aretha's 1970 hit 'Don't Play That Song (You Lied)' was originally a hit for which singer back in 1962?

13. One of Aretha Franklin's biggest-selling albums was recorded live at the New Temple Missionary Baptist Church in Los Angeles. What was it called?

14. Aretha Franklin was born in a) Memphis, Tennessee b) Macon, Georgia c) Miami, Florida?

15. Who at Atlantic Records produced her most influential work?

MARVIN GAYE

1. Which Marvin Gaye single featured two professional American footballers?

2. Which Gaye song was later covered by Kate Bush?

3. During the early 1980s, Gaye was living in which continental city?

4. Was Marvin's birth name a) Marvin Green b) Marvin Gaye c) Marvin Gay?

5. What was Marvin Gaye's biggest British hit single success as a duet with Tammi Terrell?

6. Which Motown act hit first with 'I Heard It Through The Grapevine'?

7. The co-writer of 'What's Going On' was Obie Benson, better known as a member of which hugely successful Motown vocal group?

8. Gaye wrote and sang the soundtrack for which 1972 blaxploitation film?

9. 'Mercy Mercy Me', from Marvin's 1971 album *What's Going On*, had a noteworthy subtitle. What was it?

10. So too did 'Inner City Blues'...

11. Marvin and Diana Ross enjoyed a British Top 5 hit in 1974 with 'You Are Everything', but who scored first with it three years earlier?

12. After divorcing Anna Gordy, Marvin Gaye married the woman who inspired much of the more impassioned material on his 1976 album, *I Want You*. Who was she?

13. In 1967, Marvin Gaye and Tammi Terrell charted in the States with 'Ain't No Mountain High Enough'. Who had the worldwide hit with the song in 1970?

14. Marvin's daughter from his second marriage appeared in two *Matrix* sequels. Who is she?

15. Gaye's first post-Motown hit was also his last Top 30 success. What was it?

GENESIS

1. Which was the first Genesis album to feature Phil Collins as lead vocalist?

2. *Foxtrot* was the first Genesis album to chart in Britain, hitting Number 12 in what year?

3. Phil Collins played drums on which Adam Ant Top 10 hit single?

4. Peter Gabriel released a 1980 single honouring which South African civil rights activist?

5. The genesis of Genesis took place at which Surrey-based public school?

6. What was the band's first British Top 10 single – achieved in 1978?

7. Which was the last Genesis album to feature guitarist Anthony Phillips?

8. Drummer Phil Collins made his Genesis debut on which album?

9. Mike Rutherford released his first solo album in 1980. What was it called?

10. *Duke* was recorded at ABBA's famous studio in Stockholm. What was it called?

11. During the mid 1970s, Phil Collins exorcised his jazz-rock inclinations with which band of virtuosos?

12. What is the name of the stick bass player who's been a veteran of numerous Peter Gabriel albums?

13. 'I Know What I Like (In Your Wardrobe)' was a hit for Genesis in 1974. From which album did it come?

14. Whose departure in 1977 prompted the band to call their next album ... *And Then There Were Three...*?

15. Which fellow guitarist did Steve Hackett team up with for the short-lived mid-1980s band GTR?

GEORGE HARRISON

1. A fellow Apple Records artist released a version of 'My Sweet Lord' before George Harrison. Who?

2. George Harrison produced parts of Badfinger's third album, *Straight Up*. But which aspiring US cult hero handled most of the production duties?

3. The cover photo for George Harrison's *All Things Must Pass* was taken at his vast mansion on the outskirts of Henley-on-Thames. Once a convent, what was its name?

4. What was the name of the record label formed by Harrison in 1974?

5. The first album to appear on George Harrison's Dark Horse label was *The Place I Love* in 1974 – by which group?

6. George Harrison released a seasonal single late in 1974 but it flopped. What was it called?

7. What was the first George Harrison song to feature on a Beatles record?

8. George Harrison first played a sitar on a Beatles song in 1965. What was it?

9. What song was, in a famous lawsuit, judged to have been the unconscious inspiration for Harrison's 'My Sweet Lord'?

10. Harrison's HandMade Films production company was formed in 1978 to help raise money for which film project?

11. George Harrison produced two British hit singles for the Radha Krishna Temple. 1969's 'Hare Krishna Mantra' was followed by which trance-inducing classic?

12. Harrison wrote the soundtrack to which 1968 film starring Jane Birkin?

13. George Harrison's first wife Patti Boyd had a sister Jenny who married which lanky rock drummer?

14. George immortalised a group of hardcore Beatles fans with a song in 1970. What was it?

15. 1987's 'Got My Mind Set On You', Harrison's most successful single since 'My Sweet Lord' in 1971, was originally a 1962 US single by which R&B singer?

HAWKWIND / MOTÖRHEAD

1. In the punk rock year of 1977, Motörhead knocked out a storming version of a little known 1964 Motown single by Eddie Holland. What was it?

2. What was Hawkwind's only Top 10 British album?

3. Who was the band's infamous nude dancer?

4. Which legendary drummer joined the Hawkwind ranks for 1980's *Levitation*?

5. Taking a break from Hawkwind, frontman Robert Calvert released which all-star solo concept album in 1974?

6. Which Hawkwind song has occasionally featured in the reformed Sex Pistols' live set?

7. Who was Liquid Len?

8. On which album, issued in 1971, did 'Master Of The Universe' first appear?

9. Violinist Simon House quit Hawkwind in 1978 to join which rock superstar's touring band?

10. Motörhead teamed up with Girlschool for which 1980 EP?

11. What is Lemmy's real name?

12. Nik Turner left Hawkwind in 1977 and for the next few years toured and recorded fronting which band?

13. What was the Mountain Grill, immortalised on Hawkwind's 1974 album?

14. 'Silver Machine' gave Hawkwind an unlikely a) Top 20 b) Top 10 c) Top 3 hit single in 1972.

15. During the early 1960s R&B boom, future Hawkwind mainstay Dave Brock once used to busk in the streets of Richmond, Surrey, with which later guitar legend?

JIMI HENDRIX

1. Though one of his greatest songs was the anti-war epic 'Machine Gun', Jimi Hendrix did his stint in which branch of the US military?

2. Before reaching England, Hendrix was a great admirer of the pioneering work of which Yardbirds guitarist?

3. Mitch Mitchell, the Jimi Hendrix Experience drummer, and the pre-fame David Bowie both played short stints in which mid-1960s pop combo?

4. Jimi's middle name and his favourite amplification stack were one and the same...

5. Which MOR 1966 ballad did Hendrix 'quote' during the instrumental break on 'Wild Thing' at the Monterey Pop Festival in June 1967?

6. The original sleeve for the British edition of the *Band Of Gypsys* album featured puppets of Hendrix, Bob Dylan and DJ John Peel and which other musician?

7. Controversially, Jimi's one-time New York associate Alan Douglas oversaw the addition of new instrumental parts to three posthumous album releases during the mid 1970s. What was the third and final title?

8. Hendrix famously stopped mid-song on BBC TV's *Lulu Show* and launched into 'Sunshine Of

Your Love' as a tribute to Cream. Which song, which the guitarist dismissed as 'rubbish', had been cruelly curtailed?

9. Whose distinctive bass-playing can be heard on the 15-minute 'Voodoo Chile' jam on 1968's *Electric Ladyland* album?

10. Experience bassist Noel Redding quit in 1968 to form which band?

11. Hendrix's last-ever performance took place at a festival on the Isle of Fehmarn, Germany, on 6 September 1970. The event was famously blighted by a) an electric storm b) food poisoning c) rioting Hell's Angels

12. Who was the woman with Hendrix on the night of his death on 18 September 1970?

13. Hendrix's manager, ex-Animals bassist Chas Chandler, went on to manage which hugely successful glam-era band?

14. The posthumous *In The West* album included an extraordinary live cover of Chuck Berry's 'Johnny B. Goode' – recorded at which notable Hendrix concert?

15. Ex-Jimi Hendrix Experience rhythm section drummer Mitch Mitchell and bassist Noel Redding teamed up with which West Coast guitarist for his 1972 *Kapt. Kopter And The (Fabulous) Twirly Birds* album?

IRON MAIDEN

1. Who was Iron Maiden vocalist between the years 1978 and 1981?

2. Who is the band's long-time manager and architect of the Sanctuary artist management empire?

3. Who was the artist responsible for creating 'Eddie', the Maiden mascot?

4. Which Maiden single sleeve depicted a knife-wielding Eddie crouching over Margaret Thatcher, short-skirted and prostrate on a pavement?

5. Which veteran engineer / producer oversaw Maiden's output throughout the 1980s?

6. Prior to joining Iron Maiden in 1981, Bruce Dickinson cut his teeth with which British metal act?

7. What was the band's first British Number 1 album?

8. The band's first release was a three-track EP released in 1979 on their Rock Hard label. What was the title?

9. Was an 'iron maiden' a) an instrument of torture b) an East End phrase for an uptight woman c) an early heavy metal club night?

10. What was the title of the band's second album?

11. Which storyteller wrote the original short story 'The Murders In The Rue Morgue' that inspired the 1981 Maiden song?

12. In the official video for 'The Number Of The Beast', three numbers are held up on cards in quick succession. What are they?

13. Is that Vincent Price doing the spoken-word intro to Iron Maiden's 'The Number Of the Beast'? Yes or no?

14. Which Iron Maiden album sleeve rejoiced in the iconography of Ancient Egypt – as did the subsequent tour to promote the record?

15. What was the title of the influential 1980 compilation album that featured two Iron Maiden cuts?

MICHAEL JACKSON / JACKSON 5

1. The USA For Africa all-star cast – Ray Charles, Bob Dylan and Smokey Robinson for starters – was memorable enough, but who co-wrote the 1985 chart-topping fundraiser, 'We Are The World, with Michael Jackson?

2. The Jackson 5's first four singles for Motown hit Number 1 in the USA. Which ballad, lifted from their *Third Album*, was the fourth?

3. 'Doctor My Eyes' was a British Top 10 hit for the Jackson 5 in 1972. But which US singer-songwriter wrote the song?

4. The Jackson 5's debut album was endorsed, both in its title and via a sleeve note, by which top-line Motown star?

5. Which part did Michael play in the 1978 musical *The Wiz*?

6. Which veteran of numerous film soundtracks produced 1979's *Off The Wall* and Jackson's two huge 1980s albums?

7. Which Top 3 Michael Jackson single from 1972 had previously been a 1958 hit for Bobby Day?

8. Michael Jackson was briefly married to Lisa-Marie Presley, the daughter of the King of rock 'n' roll. How long did the liaison last? a) Less

than two months b) less than a year c) less than two years

9. Paul McCartney's collaboration with Jackson on 'The Girl Is Mine' was part of an arrangement that also saw Michael duet with the ex-Beatle on which 1983 collaborative single?

10. Sometime Jackson songwriter Rod Temperton – he wrote, among others, 'Thriller' – had previously been a member of which British disco funk combo?

11. Which horror film legend contributed his distinctive speaking voice to the 'Thriller' track?

12. Which Beatles song does Jackson perform towards the end of his *Moonwalker* film?

13. The Jacksons reunited for one final album with Michael in 1984. What was the title?

14. What was Michael's first British Number 1 single?

15. Which year saw the appearance of Janet Jackson's breakthrough album, *Control*?

JETHRO TULL

1. On the band's first single, 1968's 'Sunshine Day', they were miscredited as a) Jethro b) Jethro Toe c) Jeff Rotell

2. Who quit the band at the end of 1970 to form Wild Turkey?

3. Which Tull album was presented as a spoof of a local newspaper?

4. Who was the band's drummer for most of the 1970s?

5. Which early 1970s concept record included 'The Story Of The Hare Who Lost His Spectacles'?

6. The band's synthesizer-assisted 1980 album began life as a solo project for Ian Anderson. What was it called?

7. Which Fairport Convention mainstay has also been a Tull regular since the end of the 1970s?

8. 'Serenade To A Cuckoo' was included on Tull's 1968 debut album, *This Was*, as an homage to which influential flautist and sax player?

9. Ian Anderson produced which 1974 album for Steeleye Span?

10. Blodwyn Pig were formed in 1968 by which ex-Tull guitarist?

11. Ian Anderson is an authority on which cuisine?

a) Stir fry b) sushi c) curry

12. Who played the guitar solo on the *Aqualung* title track?

13. *Thick As A Brick* was the first of two US Number 1 albums. What was the second?

14. In later years, Anderson has been newsworthy as the owner of a lucrative business in a) agricultural machinery b) salmon farms c) historical publications

15. Jethro Tull's success was crucial in establishing which new late-1960s record label?

ELTON JOHN

1. What was Elton John's first US Number 1 album?

2. For which 1983 album did Elton John fully revive his songwriting partnership with lyricist Bernie Taupin after a seven-year wobble?

3. Which 1970s Elton John single was inspired by a tennis team led by Billie Jean King?

4. When John Lennon joined Elton John on stage at Madison Square Garden in November 1974 they duetted on two Beatles songs. One was 'Lucy In The Sky With Diamonds'. The other?

5. Elton John and Bernie Taupin's 'I Can't Go On (Living Without You)' was written as a prospective 1969 Eurovision Song Contest entry for which singer?

6. Which notable 1970s Elton sideman had previously been a member of the folk rock group Magna Carta?

7. What was the Honky Chateau?

8. During his late-1970s spell away from Elton, co-songwriter Bernie Taupin worked with which theatrical rock star for a clean-up album, *From The Inside*?

9. Which early-1970s hit single was inspired by the tale of a returning Vietnam War veteran?

10. John Lennon contributed backing vocals to Elton's 1974 reworking of 'Lucy In The Sky With Diamonds' using which favoured pseudonym?

11. 'Amoureuse' was a winter 1973 hit for which Elton John collaborator?

12. 'I'm Still Standing' came from which Elton John album?

13. 'Lady Samantha' was an airplay hit for Elton in which year?

14. The 1985 hit 'Nikita' featured which 1980s singing star on backing vocals?

15. Elton guested on which British metal band's 1986 album *Rock The Nations*?

JOY DIVISION / NEW ORDER

1. Joy Division took their earlier name from which East European capital?

2. Was 'Love Will Tear Us Apart' released before or after singer Ian Curtis's suicide in May 1980?

3. Bernard Sumner later teamed up with which guitarist for the short-lived indie-dance act Electronic?

4. New Order launched in 1981 with a re-recording of a late-era Joy Division song. What was it?

5. What Werner Herzog film did Ian Curtis watch prior to his suicide?

6. What was the highest-charting New Order single during the 1980s?

7. Joy Division performed two songs on BBC TV's *Something Else* in autumn 1979. One was 'She's Lost Control'. What was the other?

8. The import-only 'Dead Souls' / 'Atmosphere' single appeared on which cult record label?

9. New Order's Gillian Gilbert is the long-time partner of which band member?

10. Ian Curtis's widow Deborah later wrote a book about her life with him. What was the title?

11. Which influential New Order single was released in 1983 on 12" only?

12. A version of which Velvet Underground song appeared on the posthumous *Still*?

13. Who managed Joy Division and New Order?

14. Factory Records boss Tony Wilson presented which mid-1970s music and arts show for Granada Television?

15. What was the first Joy Division album to hit the British Top 30?

THE KINKS

1. Ray Davies' wife sang backing vocals on numerous early Kinks records. What was her name?

2. With which North London district – immortalised by the band on album – are the Kinks best associated?

3. In which British city did drummer Mick Avory and guitarist Dave Davies have a famous on-stage bust-up in 1965?

4. The Stranglers had a Top 10 hit in 1988 with a cover of which Kinks 45?

5. Which mid-1960s Kinks single was an early foray into mantra-rock?

6. Which was the last Kinks album to feature Pete Quaife?

7. What was the full title of the Kinks' 1970 *Lola…* album?

8. What is the name of the Kinks' North London recording studio, opened in the early 1970s?

9. Ray Davies adopted which alter-ego for the series of mid-1970s *Preservation* albums?

10. Which London-based new wave act had hits with two Kinks songs?

11. What was The Kinks' last UK Number 1 single?

12. Ray Davies adopted the guise of a 1950s spiv for the video that accompanied which 1982 Kinks hit?

13. What was the title of the mid-1980s musical written and directed by Ray Davies?

14. 'Death Of A Clown' was Dave Davies's hugely successful debut single. What was the follow-up?

15. Who was the US producer behind the early Kinks sound?

KISS

1. Which KISS member adopted the 'Starchild' persona?

2. In 1978, Ace Frehley released a single, 'New York Groove', previously a Top 10 British hit for which glam pop combo?

3. KISS were the first band to sign to a new label set up by one-time Buddah Records executive Neil Bogart. What was it?

4. Who produced the 1976 album *Destroyer*?

5. In what year did Eric Carr replace Peter Criss as the band's drummer?

6. Which guitarist was on board in time for KISS's tenth anniversary tour in 1982 – and was out less than two years later?

7. Nirvana recorded which KISS song for a grunge-era tribute album of cover versions?

8. Which KISS member released a version of 'When You Wish Upon A Star'?

9. What was the title of the band's made-for-television 1978 US film?

10. Which band member was seriously injured in a car crash in 1978?

11. For which 1983 album did the group unmask themselves?

12. Who was the last of the original members to join?

13. The first US Top 20 KISS single was a live version of which song?

14. Which Phil Spector-produced classic was reworked for the 1977 *Love Gun* album?

15. All four KISS members released solo albums in 1978, though just one refrained from including a cover version. Who was he?

LED ZEPPELIN

1. The sleeve for Led Zeppelin's 1973 set, *Houses Of The Holy*, was photographed at which UK natural wonder?

2. Jimmy Page's long-standing interest in the occult prompted a liaison with which US underground film-maker for the soundtrack of *Lucifer Rising*?

3. Zeppelin launched their own record label in 1974. What was it called?

4. 1960s beat-turned-psych combo the Pretty Things were one of the first artists to sign to Zeppelin's new Swan Song label. What was the title of the resulting 1974 album?

5. Prior to joining Led Zeppelin, Robert Plant and John Bonham were part of which West Bromwich-based hippie-era outfit?

6. The band's first recording job was backing which headline-making mid-1960s balladeer?

7. Who was Led Zeppelin's notoriously hands-on manager?

8. Released in 1967, '*The Above Ground Sound*' *Of Jake Holmes* by the US singer-songwriter includes the original version of which subsequent Zeppelin signature song?

9. Which instrumental on *Led Zeppelin II* later became a vehicle for a lengthy John Bonham

drum solo in concert?

10. What was the name of the cottage in Wales where much of *Led Zeppelin III* was written?

11. Fairport Convention vocalist Sandy Denny guested on which song from Led Zeppelin's fourth album?

12. Zeppelin's 1976 concert film *The Song Remains The Same* was shot three years earlier at which notable US venue?

13. What was the name of the private jet used by Zeppelin when touring the States during the early 1970s?

14. Which was the band's last album released prior to the death of drummer John Bonham?

15. What was the name of the post-Zeppelin band formed by Robert Plant that featured both Jimmy Page and Jeff Beck on guitar?

JOHN LENNON

1. Which regular 1970s hitmakers debuted in 1969 with a reggae-flavoured cover of John Lennon's 'Give Peace A Chance'?

2. John Lennon's *Plastic Ono Band* album from 1970 is often called his 'Primal Scream' record. But who was the inspirational author of the cathartic therapy technique?

3. Which distinctive Hollywood actress took umbrage at John and Yoko baring all for their *Unfinished Music No 1: Two Virgins* album, releasing a 1969 single, 'John, You Went Too Far This Time', under the name of Rainbo?

4. The annotated childhood illustrations that graced John Lennon's 1974 set, *Walls And Bridges*, were drawn in June of which year?

5. The director of *A Hard Day's Night* and *Help!*, Richard Lester, talked John Lennon into playing Muskateer Gripweed in which 1967 film?

6. Lennon's 'Across The Universe' first appeared on a 1969 charity album. What was it called?

7. Albert Goldman published a mean-spirited biography of Lennon. What was it called?

8. In which savage 1971 song does Lennon make reference to 'Tricky Dicky', alias US President Richard Nixon?

9. Which contemporary US band recorded a version of 'I'm Losing You' with Lennon at the *Double Fantasy* sessions only to see their work left off the finished album?

10. May Pang, Lennon's companion during his infamous 'Lost Weekend', later married which notable record producer?

11. Sean Lennon was born on 9 October 1975. Which birthday was his father celebrating?

12. Which hugely successful singing star, and one-time child actress, was among the massed chorus of voices on 'Give Peace A Chance'?

13. What did John and Yoko send out to various world leaders in April 1969 to plant as symbols of peace?

14. Julian Lennon sat in on drums for which song on 1974's *Walls And Bridges* album?

15. On which album can John Lennon's 'Nutopian International Anthem' be found?

MADONNA

1.   Madonna started her career drumming for her boyfriend's band. Who were they?

2.   Madonna's status as an international superstar was assured with the completion of a 1987 world tour. What was the tour's generic title?

3.   Which 1980s album did Madonna dedicate to her then husband?

4.   Madonna was born in which US state?

5.   Prior to her solo career, Madonna danced for a French singer who enjoyed a hit in 1979 with 'Born To Be Alive'. Who was he?

6.   Madonna scored her first British Number 1 in 1985 with which single?

7.   Which US indie rock act recorded a song titled 'Into The Groove(y)' as Ciccone Youth?

8.   The 1986 film *At Close Range* featured which Madonna tie-in hit single?

9.   Madonna's first single was released in 1982. What was it called?

10.   Which up-and-coming hip hop act supported Madonna on her 1985 *Virgin Tour*?

11.   Which major musician's production company made the 1986 film *Shanghai Surprise*, featuring Madonna and her new husband Sean Penn?

12. For which album did Madonna call in her then boyfriend John 'Jellybean' Benitez to remix several of the tracks?

13. For which 1987 single did Madonna dress up as a flamenco dancer in the promo video?

14. Level 42 opened which tour for Madonna?

15. Which Madonna single stalled outside the Top 50 in 1984 only to return two years later at Number 2?

BOB MARLEY
& THE WAILERS

1. 1976's *Blackheart Man* was the first solo album by which ex-member of The Wailers?

2. Which Wailers album was originally packaged in the manner of a lift-up Zippo lighter?

3. What was the name of Marley's studio based in Kingston, Jamaica?

4. Marley's wife Rita led the vocal trio that backed the band. What was their collective name?

5. Marley was shot and wounded at his Jamaica home days before which 1976 peace concert?

6. 'One Love' was augmented with elements from which Curtis Mayfield song?

7. Marley's 1979 song 'Zimbabwe' anticipated the independence of which unilaterally declared, whites-led colonial republic?

8. Marley's version of 'I Shot The Sheriff' first appeared on which album?

9. Which Marley song, which appeared on the B-side to the 1977 'Jamming' single, was written as a nod to the emerging punk and new wave movement?

10. The mid-1960s set *The Wailing Wailers* was

recorded for whose hugely influential Studio One production/label set-up?

11. The 1975 concert album *Live!* was recorded at which central London venue?

12. Marley wrote 'Get Up, Stand Up' with which prominent member of the early 1970s Wailers?

13. Which member of the Barrett brothers rhythm section was known as 'Family Man'?

14. Which song recorded by Marley in 1967 became a hit for Johnny Nash in 1972?

15. Prior to signing with Island Records, The Wailers worked with which notable reggae producer at the start of the 1970s?

PAUL McCARTNEY

1.   The 1977 hit 'Mull Of Kintyre' was a double A-side coupled with which wildly eclipsed song?

2.   Who was Paul McCartney's first protégé at Apple Records – and the label's first non-Beatles success?

3.   McCartney's childhood home at 20 Forthlin Road, Allerton in Liverpool, is now owned by whom?

4.   The *Wild Life*-era Wings included guitarist Denny Laine and a second Denny on drums. Who was he?

5.   What was McCartney's first post-Beatles Number 1 album in Britain?

6.   Which novelty reggae-flavoured song coupled the 1972 single 'Hi Hi Hi'?

7.   The Linda McCartney-penned 'Seaside Woman' single, released in 1977, was credited to which pseudonymous group?

8.   Mid-1970s Wings guitarist Jimmy McCulloch shot to fame in 1969 with which band of one-hit wonders?

9.   What was McCartney's recorded response single to the shootings of civilians on Bloody Sunday in Northern Ireland in January 1972?

10. The distinctive violin-shaped bass that Paul McCartney has used for much of his career was manufactured by which company?

11. Who is 'Martha My Dear', on The Beatles' 1968 'White Album'?

12. In which African capital city did Wings record the 1973 album *Band On The Run*?

13. Which noted guitarist collaborated with McCartney on the 1984 single 'No More Lonely Nights'?

14. Which 1980s album featured a black and white Hollywood-style shot of Paul and Linda on the cover?

15. With which British songwriter did McCartney share most of the writing credits for the 1986 album *Press To Play*?

JONI MITCHELL

1.   Which fellow Canadian released a version of Joni Mitchell's 'The Circle Game' in 1967, three years before it appeared on *Ladies Of The Canyon*?

2.   What is Joni's birth name?

3.   Which singer's 1967 *Wildflowers* album included two songs by the then unknown Joni Mitchell?

4.   Mitchell's biggest British hit single was a song widely regarded as one of the first to raise awareness of environmental destruction. What was it?

5.   British band Nazareth rocked up which Joni album track for a 1973 hit single?

6.   Who was Mitchell's British synth-playing collaborator on her 1985 album *Dog Eat Dog*?

7.   Who was the fretless bassist who guested on several Joni Mitchell albums during the 1970s?

8.   Which acclaimed 1974 album caught Mitchell on the cusp of her transition from folk-rock towards a more jazz-influenced style?

9.   Which early Joni album featured a self-portrait on the cover?

10. Which jazz legend did Mitchell collaborate with in the late 1970s, resulting in a 1979 album that bears his name?

11. From which album came the hit single 'You Turn Me On I'm A Radio'?

12. Who produced Joni's 1968 debut album *Song To A Seagull*?

13. Which Californian Canyon, popular with LA-based musicians, is the subject of Mitchell's *Ladies Of The Canyon* album?

14. In what year did Mitchell release *The Hissing Of Summer Lawns*?

15. What, loosely, is the meaning of 'Hejira' – the title of Mitchell's 1976 album?

VAN MORRISON

1. What was Them's biggest British hit single?

2. Morrison's first solo hit, 1967's 'Brown Eyed Girl', also appeared on an album that year. What was the title of this sometimes ill-regarded affair?

3. The first song on 1972's *Saint Dominic's Preview* was a tribute to a man who was a key musical influence. What was it called?

4. Morrison came to prominence fronting Them, best known for their version of which Van original and instant garage rock classic?

5. In 1986, Morrison raided an old Them song title and created a new cut from it titled 'Here Comes The Knight'. But on which album did it appear?

6. Which artist covered 'T.B. Sheets' on his 1972 album *Never Get Out Of These Blues Alive*, which includes a guest appearance from Van?

7. Was 'Mystic Eyes' a minor hit for Them or Van Morrison as a soloist?

8. In what year was *Astral Weeks* released?

9. The US Top 10 hit 'Domino' came from which Morrison album?

10. After an absence of three years, Morrison returned in 1977 with an album co-produced by Dr John. What was it called?

11. As well as doing a duet with Richard Manuel, Morrison – backed by The Band – performed one of his best-loved songs at *The Last Waltz* concert in 1976. What was it?

12. What is Van Morrison's birth name?

13. Morrison's then wife appears on the cover of the 1971 album *Tupelo Honey*. What was her name?

14. What was the name of the large-scale band assembled by Morrison for his 1973 tour?

15. Morrison's classic live album from 1974 included a handful of Them covers as well as a ten-minute-plus version of 'Cyprus Avenue'. What was its title?

NEW YORK DOLLS

1.   The New York Dolls performed two songs on their November 1973 *OGWT* appearance. But which was their recent single?

2.   During the Dolls' late-1973 UK trip, they played two shows in the Rainbow Rooms at Biba in London. Who was the woman behind the fashion emporium?

3.   Having caught the Dolls on *OGWT*, a 14-year old in Manchester was inspired to start a fanzine dedicated to the band. What, in 1973, was his name?

4.   Which one-time Shangri-Las producer was brought on board to man the controls for the 1974 album *Too Much Too Soon*?

5.   Which future frontman of a 1980s metal band briefly replaced Johnny Thunders on a 1975 tour with the band?

6.   Johnny Thunders' band The Heartbreakers released one studio album in their lifetime. What was it called?

7.   Who, late in 1972, replaced original Dolls drummer Billy Murcia?

8.   Who, together with singer David Johansen, stayed with the Dolls virtually from start to finish?

9. What was bassist Arthur Kane's nickname?

10. What flag did manager Malcolm McLaren advise the Dolls to use as a backdrop? a) Communist hammer 'n' sickle b) Nazi swastika c) Union Jack

11. What was the title of the posthumous 1984 live album, recorded in a New York club in 1975?

12. Which British band released a track called 'Johnny Thunder' on a 1968 album?

13. Which band did Richard Hell form on leaving The Heartbreakers in 1976?

14. Buster Poindexter was a pseudonym first used by which ex-New York Doll on an eponymous 1987 solo album?

15. David Johansen's first live album included a version of 'Build Me Up Buttercup', a 1968 hit for which British club band?

PINK FLOYD

1. Which avant-garde musician collaborated with Roger Waters for the 1970 *Music From The Body* project?

2. *Relics* was a popular budget-price Pink Floyd album during the 1970s. But what was its less-remembered subtitle?

3. What was the name of David Gilmour's pre-Floyd Cambridge-based combo?

4. Which Syd Barrett girlfriend and 1960s Quorum model was 'Jennifer Gentle' in the 1967 Floyd song 'Lucifer Sam'?

5. Early Pink Floyd producer Norman Smith enjoyed two Top 10 hits in the early 1970s under the name Hurricane Smith. The first was 'Don't Let It Die'. What was the second?

6. Which late-1960s underground band muddled its way through 'No Good Trying' on Syd Barrett's 1970 debut solo album, *The Madcap Laughs*?

7. Who owned Seamus, the dog that howled its way through a song on the Floyd's 1971 album, *Meddle*?

8. Under what title did 'Careful With That Axe, Eugene' appear in reworked form on the soundtrack to Michelangelo Antonioni's 1970 film *Zabriskie Point*?

9. Whose voice graced 'The Great Gig In The Sky' on the Floyd's 1973 epic, *The Dark Side Of The Moon*?

10. 'Raving And Drooling' was one of three new songs premiered by the band at a series of shows in 1974. It later turned up on *Animals* under which title?

11. Floyd bassist and concept man Roger Waters famously spat at a fan during a show on the band's 1977 North American tour. It sparked the initial inspiration for what would become *The Wall*, but in which city did the unsavoury incident take place?

12. Which member of Pink Floyd produced The Damned's second album, 1977's *Music For Pleasure*?

13. Floyd keyboard player Rick Wright formed a side project with Dave Harris from Fashion. What was it called?

14. Which Roger Waters solo album featured an illustration of a naked girl with a rucksack on her back?

15. What was the name of the noteworthy design team responsible for many Pink Floyd album covers?

THE POLICE

1.   Prior to joining The Police, Stewart Copeland did a stint with which early-1970s British pop-prog outfit?

2.   The Police's 'Every Breath You Take' provided the sonic backdrop to Puff Daddy's 1997 tribute single to his murdered protégé, Notorious B.I.G. What was the song?

3.   How did Gordon Sumner acquire the name 'Sting'?

4.   What was the first Police album to feature an English-language title?

5.   The Police's 1981 album, *Ghost In The Machine*, took its title from a book by which celebrated 20th-century thinker?

6.   Initially, The Police had a second guitarist. Who was he?

7.   The group's manager was also the drummer's brother. Who was he?

8.   What 1979 single gave The Police their first British Number 1?

9.   Which Police single name-checks *Lolita* author Vladimir Nabakov?

10. Who produced the first three Police albums?

11. What role did Sting play in the 1979 film version

of *Quadrophenia*?

12. For what 1984 film was Sting obliged to dye his hair orange?

13. What was the title of Sting's 1985 debut solo album?

14. Which future Police man was part of short-lived acid-rock outfit Dantalian's Chariot?

15. Which member of The Police grew up in the Middle East thanks to his father's role in the CIA?

IGGY POP / THE STOOGES

1. There were two Asheton brothers in The Stooges. Which one was the drummer?

2. What's Iggy's real name?

3. How did he get his Iggy name?

4. Which Stooges song was covered by the Sex Pistols for the B-side of their 1977 'Pretty Vacant' single?

5. 'Raw Power' was written by Iggy Pop together with which member of The Stooges?

6. On which 1970s Stooges album did 'Cock In My Pocket' feature?

7. Iggy's cover of Johnny O'Keefe's late 1950s rock 'n' roll hit 'The Wild One' gave him a British Top 10 hit single, albeit with a reworked title. What was it?

8. 'China Girl', later a hit for co-writer David Bowie, first appeared on which Iggy Pop album?

9. Which British post-punk band had a minor hit with their 1987 version of 'The Passenger'?

10. Iggy's 1980 *Soldier* album boasted which ex-Sex Pistol in its credits?

11. Which ex-Sex Pistol co-wrote three songs with

Iggy for the 1986 hit album *Blah-Blah-Blah*?

12. By what name were The Stooges known in their early days?

13. The Stooges were signed to Elektra in 1968 on the recommendation of the label's legendarily golden-eared publicist. Who was he?

14. After The Stooges disbanded in the mid 1970s, which Asheton brother teamed up with the Detroit-based Destroy All Monsters?

15. Who produced the first Stooges album?

ELVIS PRESLEY

1. After a successful television 'Comeback Special', Elvis Presley returned to concert performance in which year?

2. Chips Moman produced which career-changing 1969 Elvis album?

3. What was the theme tune for Elvis's 1968 'Comeback Special' – a finale for the show and released as a tie-in single?

4. With which song did Elvis's 1970s show almost always end?

5. The 1970 live album *On Stage* was recorded at which Las Vegas hotel, the venue for several Presley concert seasons?

6. Who designed Elvis's vast wardrobe of 1970s jumpsuits?

7. Who was the extraordinarily deep-voiced singer who, with his gospel group The Stamps, regularly backed Elvis during the 1970s?

8. Which legendary rock 'n' roll guitarist joined Elvis's backing group in 1969 and stayed with him until Presley's death in 1977?

9. Elvis's personal physician Dr George Nichopoulos was better known by which name?

10. By what name were Elvis Presley's inner circle of friends and bodyguards known?

11. A book written by three of his closest associates, and published weeks before his death, made public the less savoury aspects of Presley's personal life. What was it called?

12. Within days of Presley's death, his latest, largely ignored single shot to the top of the British charts. What was it called?

13. During which song did Elvis get a fit of the giggles while performing in Vegas, a recording subsequently known as 'The Laughing Version'?

14. In which year did Presley make his unprecedented worldwide satellite concert broadcast from Hawaii?

15. Elvis's passion for which martial art gets an airing in the 1972 documentary film *Elvis On Tour*? a) Tai chi b) Karate c) Kung fu

PRINCE

1. In which year did Prince first suggest we party like it was 1999?

2. What is Prince's birth name?

3. 'Love Song' was a duet written and recorded with which similarly successful 1980s performer?

4. Prince's debut album, released in 1978, was largely overlooked. What was it called?

5. What is Prince's hometown?

6. The first non-Prince album on his Paisley Park label imprint was titled *Romance 1600*. Who was the artist?

7. The enormous success of the *Purple Rain* film prompted a follow-up directed by and starring Prince. What was it called?

8. His US Number 1 hit 'Kiss' first appeared on which Prince album?

9. Prince duetted with which Scottish singer for the 1987 single 'U Got The Look'?

10. Which female vocal duo accompanied Prince on much of his 1980s work before releasing self-titled albums such as *Fruit At The Bottom* and *Eroica*?

11. What was Prince's first British Top 10 single?

12. Which band, featuring singer Morris Day, did Prince mentor during the early 1980s?

13. Which 1986 hit single did Prince write for the Bangles?

14. Prince originally wrote 'Nothing Compares 2 U' for which mid-1980s side project?

15. Which hit single contained a recitation of the Lord's Prayer midway through the song?

QUEEN

1. 'Bohemian Rhapsody' was Queen's first British Number 1 single – but in which year?

2. Freddie Mercury studied graphic design in which notable London art school where previous students included Pete Townshend and Ronnie Wood?

3. What was the name of Brian May's pre-Queen band, with Roger Taylor on drums and fronted by Tim Staffell?

4. *Fun In Space* was a 1981 solo album by which Queen member?

5. Freddie Mercury was born on which island off the coast of East Africa?

6. What was Queen's first single, released in 1973?

7. What was Queen's second Number 1 British hit single?

8. Which band member wrote 'Radio Ga Ga'?

9. Which 1978 album was the last produced with Roy Thomas Baker?

10. 'Fat Bottomed Girls' was a 1978 double A-sided single together with which song?

11. By what name is Brian May's custom-made guitar, which he's used since the late 1960s, commonly known?

12. On which album did the song 'Sheer Heart Attack' appear?

13. Queen performed the soundtrack for which 1980 sci-fi film?

14. What was the name of Queen's first live album, released in 1979?

15. Freddie Mercury's first solo single, 'Love Kills', was a collaboration with Giorgio Moroder for the soundtrack of which silent film classic?

LOU REED / THE VELVET UNDERGROUND

1.   Lou Reed's *Metal Machine Music*, first released in 1975, sounds no less tuneful decades later. But how did he create it?

2.   Lou Reed's 'Perfect Day', a British Number 1 in 1997 thanks to a BBC-assembled all-star cast, originally appeared on which album?

3.   On which Velvet Underground album could be found the drone-rock epic 'Sister Ray'?

4.   There were probably several reasons why the authorities wanted to silence the Velvet Underground's 1967 debut album, not least for its at times shockingly abrasive sound, but titling one song after a notorious illegal drug broke a taboo. What was the song?

5.   Which John Cale album included musical extrapolations on a couple of poems by actor/ writer Sam Shepard?

6.   What was the name of Andy Warhol's Manhattan art studio?

7.   Who was 'Jackie' in Lou Reed's 'Walk On The Wild Side'?

8.   Gerard Malanga danced on stage with the Velvet Underground while wielding a) a whip b) a vibrator c) a flower

9. Who was John Cale's collaborator on the 1971 album *The Church Of Anthrax*?

10. Which latter-day Lou Reed collaborator recorded several Velvet Underground shows that were later given official release as part of a 'Bootleg Series'?

11. What was the title of Lou Reed's 1974 live album?

12. John Cale, Nico and Eno performed at the A.C.N.E. concert at London's Rainbow Theatre on 1 June 1974. But which musician provided the A part of the acronym?

13. Which was the first Velvet Underground album to chart in Britain?

14. Chelsea Girls was a) a song b) a film c) both?

15 In which year did the classic Velvet Underground line-up reform for a European tour?

R.E.M.

1. R.E.M.'s first single was released in 1981. What was it?

2. The band turned to which producer, best known for his work with British folk rock and psychedelic acts, for their third album, *Fables Of The Reconstruction*?

3. What was the 1987 album made up of rarities and B-sides from their early career?

4. In what year did Michael Stipe shave his head to look, in his words, like Marlon Brando?

5. Michael Stipe guested on 'A Campfire Song' on which band's 1987 album, *In My Tribe*?

6. What was the name of the band's 1982 debut EP?

7. What was the first of several R.E.M. albums that saw Scott Litt in the production credits?

8. Which ex-member quit the group in 1997 to become a farmer?

9. 'Strange', on 1987's *Document* album, was a cover version of a song by which British post-punk band?

10. Which 1980s R.E.M. side project has featured Warren Zevon on vocals?

11. What was the band's first British Top 20 hit single?

12. Which city is home for R.E.M.?

13. The band released a cover of 'Toys In The Attic' on the flip of 'Fall On Me'. Who did the original?

14. Michael Stipe sang vocals on a cover of Moby Grape's 'Omaha' on *Visions Of Excess*, a 1985 set featuring an all-star cast by which US muso combo?

15. R.E.M. released the first of numerous fan club singles in a) 1984 b) 1986 c) 1988?

THE ROLLING STONES

1. Brian Jones spent his final months living in the former country home of which noted British children's writer?

2. She sang the distinctive support vocal on 'Gimme Shelter'. Who was she?

3. Keith's beau Anita Pallenberg starred alongside Mick Jagger in the 1970 film *Performance*. Who was the other woman in the ménage-a-trois?

4. Much of *Exile On Main St.* was recorded at Nellcôte, Keith Richards' hideaway in the Côte d'Azur region of southern France. What was the name of the boat he used during breaks from the makeshift basement studio?

5. Mick Taylor received a rare co-writer's credit on the *It's Only Rock 'n' Roll* album. For which song?

6. Bill Wyman was the first Stone to release a bona fide solo album. What was it called?

7. *Metamorphosis*, released in 1975, was a rare venture into the archives by the Rolling Stones. But which Stevie Wonder cover was lifted from it for a tie-in 45?

8. In a 1975 BBC radio documentary, which Stone claimed that he disliked touring because he hated leaving his family?

9. Ron Wood officially became a Rolling Stone in 1976. Ten years earlier, he was playing guitar with which struggling beat combo?

10. 'Cherry Oh Baby', on 1976's *Black And Blue* album, was hardly the most distinguished rock cover of a reggae song. Who fared better on the original?

11. The Stones' 1978 single 'Miss You' marked a triumphant return to form. Who played the song's distinctive harp part?

12. Mick Jagger and Keith Richards suffered a major falling out during the making of which 1980s Stones album?

13. The Stones lost their long-serving keyboard player Ian Stewart in which year?

14. What, according to Bill Wyman, was Stu's favourite phrase for the band, most often uttered as the band were about to go on stage?

15. One of several guitarists considered to replace Mick Taylor in the Rolling Stones was Harvey Mandel. With which band had he made his name?

DIANA ROSS

1. Diana Ross was nominated for an Academy Award for her portrayal of Billie Holiday in which 1972 biopic?

2. Diana Ross got separate billing with The Supremes in which year?

3. 'Missing You', written by Lionel Richie, was Diana's tribute to which Motown colleague?

4. The final Diana Ross And The Supremes single was a US Number 1 over the 1969 Christmas holiday. What was it?

5. 'I'm Still Waiting' was Ross's first British Number 1, but from which album was it lifted?

6. Which song, another US Number 1 single, was the Ross-sung theme for a 1975 feature film produced by Motown?

7. Which 1979 album reunited Diana with her early producers?

8. Ross made a successful crossover into the disco market with which 1980 album, produced by Chic's Nile Rodgers and Bernard Edwards?

9. 'Endless Love', a 1981 duet with Lionel Richie, was the theme for which Franco Zeffirelli film?

10. Who were the songwriting/production team that engineered Ross's early success as a solo artist?

11. What was the 1985 Diana Ross album masterminded by the Gibb brothers?

12. What was the name of Diana's mid-1970s one-woman show?

13. After parting company from Motown, Ross spent much of the 1980s with which record label?

14. Which group received guest-star billing on *Diana!*, Ross's 1971 US television special?

15. What was Diana Ross's first solo single?

ROXY MUSIC AND ENO

1. Whistling appeared on which Roxy Music single?

2. Which Roxy Music album cover features the then girlfriend of Can guitarist Michael Karoli (and his cousin)?

3. Brian Eno lent his support to which slightly out of tune 1970s orchestra?

4. A late-1973 precursor of the Sex Pistols took its name from which Roxy Music song?

5. What was the title of Andy Mackay's 1974 solo album?

6. Who did Phil Manzanera replace in Roxy Music early in 1972?

7. Prior to joining Roxy Music in 1973, violinist Eddie Jobson had been a member of which progressive rock band?

8. What was the influential management team behind the band's breakthrough and subsequent career?

9. What was the band's follow-up single to 'Virginia Plain'?

10. Which London fashion designer was the stylist for a string of Roxy Music album covers?

11. What was Roxy Music's first British Number 1 album?

12. Bryan Ferry re-recorded four songs from the first Roxy Music album for which solo record?

13. Mid-1970s Roxy Music bassist John Gustafson started his career with two Merseybeat bands. Name one of them.

14. Bryan Ferry's then girlfriend Jerry Hall appeared on the cover of which Roxy Music album?

15. Which post-punk-era Roxy album kicked off with a cover version of Wilson's Pickett's 'In The Midnight Hour'?

SANTANA

1.   Santana's career revived with a cover of The Zombies' 1964 hit 'She's Not There', taken from which tie-in double album?

2.   Carlos Santana collaborated with Mahavishnu Orchestra guitarist John McLaughlin for which 1973 album?

3.   Early Santana keyboard player Gregg Rolie formed a mid-1970s jazz rock band that, by 1980, had transformed into one of the world's leading AOR acts. Who were they?

4.   Which furiously paced instrumental helped make Santana the stars of the *Woodstock* film?

5.   Though a Top 5 US hit for Santana in 1970, 'Black Magic Woman' had been a minor hit for Fleetwood Mac two years earlier. Who wrote the song?

6.   Which instrumental, a highlight of the 1970 *Abraxas* album, has since become a Carlos Santana signature tune?

7.   Which 1970s Santana album sported a butterfly on its shiny blue sleeve?

8.   The 1974 album *Illuminations* was a collaboration between Carlos Santana and which jazz musician?

9.   In 1983, Carlos Santana released a solo album

that mainly consisted of cover versions. What was it called?

10. Though mainman Carlos was born in Mexico, from which US city did Santana emerge during the late 1960s?

11. On the back of their successful appearance at the Woodstock Festival in August 1969, Santana scored a US Top 10 hit single months later with which song from their debut album?

12. 'Oye Como Va', an early band classic, was originally written and performed by the so-called 'King of Latin music'. Who was he?

13. 1972 saw the release of a live collaboration between Carlos Santana and a one-time Electric Flag drummer more recently known for his short-lived association with Jimi Hendrix. Who was he?

14. Santana broke out stylistically in 1972 with a more jazz-influenced instrumental approach for their fourth studio album. What was it called?

15. Who was the spiritual master whose teachings informed the collaboration with John McLaughlin and which Carlos Santana followed for much of the 1970s?

SEX PISTOLS

1. Television presenter Bill Grundy inadvertently helped propel the Pistols to the front pages in December 1976 after their appearance on Thames TV's *Today* programme. But which post-punk band asked, in 1978, 'Where's Bill Grundy Now'?

2. The Sex Pistols' graphics designer Jamie Reid was influenced by which late 1950/1960s art and culture movement?

3. During Jubilee Week 1977, the Sex Pistols' 'God Save The Queen' was pipped in most charts for the Number 1 spot by which record?

4. Between Let It Rock and SEX, Malcolm McLaren and Vivienne Westwood's Kings Road fashion emporium was known by what name?

5. During 1976, Johnny Rotten and Sid Vicious shared a squat in an otherwise fashionable corner of North London. Where?

6. Inspired by the success of his mates, Sid Vicious formed a band late in 1976, its name later reprised as the title of a single by the John Lydon-fronted PiL.

7. A loose studio demo of the Small Faces' 'What'cha Gonna Do About It' appeared on the 1978 *Great Rock 'n' Roll Swindle* album. But what Small Faces B-side did the band sometimes perform live during 1976?

8. An early Sex Pistols demo session was recorded in May 1976 at Majestic Studios. The producer was which well-known guitarist and session man?

9. Which progressive-era band did Johnny Rotten cite as an influence during a 1977 Capital Radio show?

10. The Pistols played several dates in August 1977 incognito in a short tour known as SPOTS. What did the acronym stand for?

11. Weeks before the release of the *Never Mind The Bollocks* album, a spoiler bootleg LP containing earlier, raw versions of the material sold in vast quantities. Its title?

12. Rich Kids was the name of bassist Glen Matlock's post-Pistols band and debut single. What was the title of the band's debut album?

13. What was the bawdy nautical song included in the *Great Rock 'n' Roll Swindle* film?

14. Despite its threadbare nature, a collage-style interview album managed a Top 10 placing in 1979. What was it called?

15. In 1979, Sex Pistols drummer Paul Cook and guitarist Steve Jones formed which hard-rockin', two-album combo?

SIOUXSIE
AND THE BANSHEES

1.   T. Rex's '20th Century Boy' and The Beatles'
     'Helter Skelter' used to appear in early Siouxsie
     And The Banshees set-lists. So too did a theme
     from which Supermarionated 1960s kids TV
     programme?

2.   Between playing with Siouxsie And The
     Banshees at their 1976 100 Club debut and
     joining Adam And The Ants at the start of 1980,
     guitarist Marco Pirroni was in two groups.
     Name one of them?

3.   The Banshees grew out of which South-East
     London suburb?

4.   Guitarist John McGeoch joined the group from
     which new wave act?

5.   What was the title of the Banshees' collection of
     cover versions released in 1987?

6.   'The Lord's Prayer', performed at the group's
     100 Club debut in 1976, was reworked for
     which album?

7.   Which 1981 single shared its title with an Alfred
     Hitchcock film from 1945?

8.   The Cure's Robert Smith guested on one
     Banshees studio album. Which was it?

9. In 1982, Steven Severin and Robert Smith embarked on a short-lived neo-psychedelic side project. What was it called?

10. 'Supernatural Thing', the B-side to 'Arabian Knights', was a cover of a mid-1970s song by which US soul singer?

11. Banshees drummer Budgie had previously been in which Liverpool-based band with Holly Johnson and singer Jane Casey?

12. Steven Severin produced the first records by which Scottish post-punk band?

13. 1986's *Tinderbox* featured which guitarist?

14. 'This Wheel's On Fire', a 1987 hit single for the Banshees in 1987, was previously a late 1960s hit for which act?

15. What was the name of the drummer who played on the first two Banshees albums?

SLY AND THE FAMILY STONE

1. Sly Stone cut his teeth as a producer for a small San Francisco-based label, Autumn Records, working with Grace Slick in her pre-Jefferson Airplane outfit. Who were they?

2. Sly And The Family Stone's 1970 hit 'Thank You (Falettinme Be Mice Elf Agin)', was covered a decade later by which British new wave band?

3. Sly Stone released his first solo album in 1975. What was it called?

4. Who was the band's second singer / keyboard player / platinum wig wearer?

5. What is Sly Stone's birth name?

6. Who was the band's bassist, often credited with popularising the 'slap bass' technique?

7. Which early 1969 US Number 1 single utilised the popular phrase, 'Different strokes for different folks'?

8. Post-punk band The Raincoats covered which hit single lifted from the 1971 album *There's A Riot Goin' On*?

9. A rare cover version, all the more surprising because it was a song popularised by Doris Day, appeared on the 1973 album *Fresh*. What was it?

10. Sly Stone formed the band with his guitar-playing brother. What was his name?

11. How many Top 30 albums did Sly And The Family Stone achieve in Britain? a) One b) Three c) None

12. On 5 June 1974, Sly Stone got married in a very public place. Where?

13. What was the band's only Top 10 British single?

14. Which Sly And The Family Stone album included the hits 'Everyday People' and 'I Want To Take You Higher'?

15. Sly Stone collaborated on which band's 1981 album, *The Electric Spanking Of War Babies*?

PATTI SMITH

1. Patti Smith's 1974 debut 45 coupled an original, 'Piss Factory', with a cover of which rock standard?

2. In 1972, Patti Smith Group guitarist Lenny Kaye compiled a two-disc anthology of mid-1960s garage rock. What was its full title?

3. The final song on 1975's *Horses* was 'Elegie'. To whom was it dedicated?

4. Patti Smith's two nights at London's Roundhouse in May 1976 marked a key moment in the switch from old wave to new wave. But which up-and-coming homegrown anti-heroes provided support?

5. Which cover version did Smith famously preface with a 'Tick, tock, fuck the clock' spoken-word intro at her mid-70s concerts?

6. *Radio Ethiopia* producer Jack Douglas later produced what turned out to be a legendary swansong album at New York's Hit Factory studio. For whom?

7. At what studio was Patti Smith's debut album *Horses* recorded?

8. Which experimental US duo released a song, 'Patti Smith', that appeared – optimistically – on a chart-eluding triple album?

9. In 1971, Patti wrote and performed a play, *Cowboy Mouth*, with which future prize-winning playwright and actor?

10. Which band, in 1981, released an album that took its title from a Patti Smith song, 'Fire Of Unknown Origin'?

11. Smith's first 45 included a version of 'Hey Joe' that began with a spoken-word piece inspired by which newsworthy heiress?

12. Smith's 1979 single 'Frederick' was dedicated to her partner and ex-MC5 guitarist. Who was he?

13. Which 1967 film inspired a key song – subtitled 'Set Me Free' – on the 1978 album *Easter*?

14. What was the title of Smith's first notable volume of poetry, published in 1972?

15. After a nine-year hiatus since her previous studio album, Smith returned in 1988 with a fifth set. Its title?

THE SMITHS

1. Producer Stephen Street's induction with the band came as engineer for which 1984 Smiths single?

2. A newly wealthy woman graced the sleeve of 'Heaven Knows I'm Miserable Now'. Who was she?

3. The Smiths started life with which leading independent record label?

4. Which local guitarist and future 1980s indie rock notable did the pre-Smiths Morrissey briefly appear alongside with Manchester band The Nosebleeds?

5. Johnny Marr shares a birth name with another Mancunian musician. Who is he?

6. Who joined the band in 1986, making The Smiths a five-piece?

7. Who appeared on the cover of the *Louder Than Bombs* compilation?

8. The posthumous live album *Rank* was recorded in which year?

9. Which British rock 'n' roller appeared on the cover of The Smiths' 1987 single 'Last Night I Dreamt That Somebody Loved Me'?

10. Who was Morrissey's main musical collaborator on his 1988 solo debut, *Viva Hate*?

11. Famously, Morrissey's first gig as a young teenager was seeing which early 1970s pop sensations?

12. During the early 1980s, Morrissey had a small book published about which 1950s Hollywood legend?

13. The 'man in a mirrored puddle' image that graced the sleeve for the 'This Charming Man' single was a still from which 1950 French film?

14. Which 1985 Smiths single was refashioned into a band name by ex-Bananarama singer Siobhan Fahey?

15. Alain Delon appears on the cover of which Smiths record?

BRUCE SPRINGSTEEN

1. 'Jungleland' closes which classic Springsteen album?

2. What, famously, was Springsteen's four-track album?

3. Which E Street Band musician does Bruce Springsteen lean against on the cover of his 1975 *Born To Run* album?

4. Who was the E Street Band drummer turned television personality?

5. Which Springsteen sideman played Silvio Dante in the TV series *The Sopranos*?

6. Who is Springsteen's musician wife?

7. Which influential A&R man signed Springsteen to Columbia Records in 1972?

8. What was Springsteen's first British Number 1 album?

9. Which young actress appeared alongside Springsteen in the promo video for 1984's 'Dancing In The Dark'?

10. Which 1980 single had originally been written for The Ramones?

11. Jon Landau, Springsteen's collaborator and co-producer of many of his major albums, cut his teeth as a rock critic for which US magazine?

12. Which guitarist, an established artist in his own right, joined Springsteen's E Street Band in 1984?

13. At which venue did Springsteen make his London debut in November 1975?

14. The Pointer Sisters had a Top 3 US hit single early in 1979 with which then unreleased Springsteen song?

15. 1978's 'The Promised Land' pays homage to a similarly named song by which 1950s rock 'n' roll legend?

RINGO STARR

1. Who had the original hit in 1960 with 'You're Sixteen', a 1974 success for Ringo Starr?

2. When asked in *A Hard Day's Night* whether he is a Mod or a Rocker, how does Ringo describe himself?

3. What was Ringo's songwriting contribution to the *Abbey Road* album?

4. Ringo's drumming forerunner in The Beatles was a) Rory Storm b) Pete Best c) Stuart Sutcliffe?

5. Which drummer replaced Ringo for a series of Beatles concerts in June 1964 while Starr was recovering from illness?

6. Which children's television series did Ringo narrate during the mid 1980s?

7. With what song does Ringo conclude the Beatles' 'White Album'?

8. Which Ringo album depicted an old Merseyside pub on the front cover?

9. Starr's 1973 hit 'Photograph' was a co-write with which ex-Beatle?

10. Ringo met his second wife, Barbara Bach, on the set of a film they were both starring in. What was it?

11. In the 1973 film *That'll Be The Day*, Ringo was

reunited with which Liverpool-based singer from his days drumming with Rory Storm And The Hurricanes?

12. Which song did Ringo sing at the August 1971 Concert For Bangla Desh?

13. In 1972, Starr directed which film starring Marc Bolan?

14. What was Ringo's highest-charting British hit single?

15. Which song did John Lennon write for inclusion on Ringo's self-titled 1973 solo album?

ROD STEWART
/ THE FACES

1. Rod Stewart's version of Jimi Hendrix's 'Angel' was a big hit in 1972. But from which of the guitarist's albums was the song taken?

2. Rod Stewart's 'Sailing' was a huge hit in autumn 1975. But which band did it first?

3. What was the name of the Japanese-born bassist who replaced Ronnie Lane in The Faces in 1973?

4. Rod Stewart's debut solo album kicked off with a cover of which Rolling Stones song?

5. Where was Rod Stewart born?

6. Rod's predecessor, Small Faces frontman Steve Marriott, formed which rock supergroup in 1969?

7. The hugely successful 1971 single 'Maggie May' was coupled with a cover of which Tim Hardin song?

8. 'This Old Heart Of Mine', a 1975 hit for Rod Stewart, was originally a mid-1960s hit for which US soul act?

9. DJ John Peel accompanied The Faces on a *Top of the Pops* appearance, miming to the mandolin part. But which Lindisfarne member played it on the record?

10. The 1972 hit 'Stay With Me' was lifted from which Faces album?

11. Which member of The Faces turned his nose up at a Small Faces mid-1970s reunion?

12. What was Rod's next chart-topper after 'Maggie May'?

13. Which mid-1960s soul revue-style band featured Rod Stewart alongside Long John Baldry and Julie Driscoll?

14. In 1983, Stewart was back on top of the British singles chart again with which song?

15. What was The Faces' only Number 1 British album?

10cc

1. Pre-10cc band Hotlegs had a one-off hit in 1970 with which mantra-like song?

2. Graham Gouldman was inadvertently responsible for Eric Clapton's departure from The Yardbirds, when the guitarist deemed one of the young songwriter's songs too pop for a self-respecting R&B group. It became the band's first Top 3 hit... Which song was it?

3. Which Yardbirds hit was not written by Gouldman?

4. Gouldman met future 10cc guitarist Eric Stewart when in 1968 he joined a band best known for their 1966 hit 'A Groovy Kind Of Love'. Who were they?

5. What was the name of the recording studio in Stockport used extensively by 10cc and, later, punk acts such as Buzzcocks and Joy Division?

6. Whose falsetto voice graced 10cc's breakthrough 45, 1972's 'Donna'?

7. Which songwriting pairing wrote 10cc's biggest hit, 1975's 'I'm Not In Love'?

8. 10cc's final British Top 10 hit was a reggae-inspired Number 1 hit in autumn 1978. What was it called?

9. 'The Wall Street Shuffle' was the lead-off song on

which 10cc album, issued in 1974?

10. When did Godley and Creme quit 10cc?

11. Which 1980s promo video did the prolific and innovative production team of Godley and Creme not shoot? a) The Police's 'Every Breath You Take' b) Frankie Goes To Hollywood's 'Two Tribes' c) Adam and the Ants' 'Prince Charming'

12. 10cc's early 1970s work was issued via a UK label run by which singer turned entertainment impresario?

13. What was the last 10cc album to feature the classic four-piece line-up?

14. What guitar effect, which could create a symphonic-like sound, was invented in the early 1970s by Kevin Godley and Lol Creme?

15. Which 10cc member produced the Ramones' 1981 album, *Pleasant Dreams*?

TRAFFIC

1. Which member of Traffic released the *Alone Together* solo album in 1970?

2. To which English county did Traffic famously retreat in 1967?

3. What, until their 1990s reunion, was the last Traffic album?

4. What was the title of Steve Winwood's hugely successful 1986 album?

5. Which 1967 film starred Barry Evans and Judy Geeson and featured a title track performed by Traffic?

6. Steve Winwood came to prominence singing which early 1966 hit for the Spencer Davis Group?

7. Which Traffic song quickly became a Joe Cocker stage favourite?

8. What was the title of Traffic's sprawling 1973 live double album?

9. What was the band's post-Blind Faith reunion album?

10. What is the name of Steve Winwood's elder brother, one-time Spencer Davis Group bassist and latter-day music biz executive?

11. Which band member wrote 'Hole In My Shoe'?

12. What was Traffic's highest-charting British album?

13. Which band member released a 1971 collaborative album with Cass Elliot?

14. Who embarked on a solo career with the 1972 solo album *Oh How We Danced*?

15. What was the title of the Spencer Davis Group's first album without Steve Winwood?

U2

1. Which U2 song was written in tribute to the late US Civil Rights leader Martin Luther King?

2. What is the Edge's real name?

3. What was the band's debut release for Island?

4. Who has been the band's long-term manager?

5. What was the lead song on the band's three-track debut EP, *Three*?

6. What is the title of U2's first live album?

7. Bono spars vocally with which US rock legend on 'Sweet Fire Of Love' from the latter's self-titled 1987 solo album?

8. Which was the first album with Brian Eno in the producer's chair?

9. What was the band's first British chart-topping album?

10. U2 associate Gavin Friday once fronted which theatrically inclined post-punk band?

11. What is Bono's real name?

12. What was the title of the Edge's 1986 soundtrack album?

13. What is popularly known as 'the U2 studio' in Dublin?

14. U2 didn't have a British Number 1 single until 1988. What was the song that did it?

15. In which US state lies the Joshua Tree National Park?

PAUL WELLER / THE JAM

1. The Jam covered Ray Davies' 'David Watts' for a 1978 single. But on which Kinks album did the song first appear?

2. What was the debut Jam 45?

3. The Jam's 1977 debut album, *In The City*, included a version of the *Batman* theme and 'Slow Down', the latter a cover of a song by which 1950s rocker?

4. Paul Weller's Style Council collaborator Mick Talbot cut his teeth with which mod revival band?

5. Which chart-topping Jam single from 1982 was written by Weller with his home town Woking in mind?

6. After The Jam folded, bassist Bruce Foxton spent more than a decade with which enduring punk-era band?

7. The Jam peaked early in 1980 when which single flew straight into Number 1?

8. In which Mod-related town did The Jam play their farewell concert?

9. Which Style Council backing singer became Weller's wife?

10. What was the title of Weller's 1984 song,

credited to the Council Collective, released in support of striking miners?

11. Which album was rejected by Polydor in 1989, prompting the Style Council to call it a day?

12. The Style Council scored their only British Number 1 album in 1985. What was it called?

13. Who was the Weller protégé who had a 1983 hit with 'The House That Jack Built'?

14. The Style Council's 1984 album *Café Blue* was given a different title for the US market. What was it?

15. What was the title of The Jam's 1983 compilation album?

THE WHO

1. The Who's reputation on the West London mod scene was ignited during their 1964 residency at which Harrow hostelry?

2. Drummer Keith Moon had previously played with which West London-based covers band?

3. The Who's debut 45, 'I'm The Face', appeared on which record label?

4. The Who's management team was Kit Lambert and Chris Stamp. Both had famous siblings. Name one of them.

5. Which Who single ends with Pete Townshend exclaiming, 'I saw ya!'

6. A cover of The Who's 'So Sad About Us' featured on the flip of which Jam single?

7. At which notable Who show did Pete Townshend tell Yippie radical Abbie Hoffman to 'Get off my fucking stage'?

8. What role did 'Crazy World Of' singer Arthur Brown play in the 1975 film version of *Tommy*?

9. What single were The Who promoting on *Top of the Pops* in 1973 when, at the end of their appearance, they smashed instruments out of frustration at the programme's lack of organisation?

10. What was The Who's last Top 10 British hit single?

11. Parts of The Who's *Who's Next* and the Stones' *Exile On Main St.* were sketched out at Mick Jagger's country house in Berkshire. What was its name?

12. The Who's *Tommy* was an album, a tour, a film and a stage production. What was the surname of its central character?

13. Who drew the cartoon cover for *The Who By Numbers*?

14. Which Who member inspired Jimmy Page to call his new band Led Zeppelin?

15. What was The Who's only chart-topping album in Britain?

STEVIE WONDER

1. Malcolm Cecil and Robert Margouleff were instrumental in assisting Stevie Wonder's turn towards synthesizers during the early 1970s. The pair were far better known by their collective name. What was it?

2. Stevie Wonder's 'Sir Duke' was a tribute to which US jazz legend?

3. What was the title of Stevie Wonder's 1980 hit single written as a nod to Bob Marley?

4. Which 1976 Stevie Wonder song became the musical basis for Coolio's 1995 hit 'Gangsta's Paradise'?

5. For which British guitar hero did Stevie Wonder originally write 'Superstition'?

6. What was Stevie Wonder's first solo British Number 1 single?

7. 'I Just Called To Say I Love You' featured on the soundtrack of which 1984 romantic comedy directed by and starring Gene Wilder?

8. Which Stevie Wonder single was written to raise awareness of a campaign to make the day of Martin Luther King's birth a national holiday?

9. In which US state was Stevie Wonder born?

10. What was the instrument, hugely popular in

early 1970s funk, that dominated the sound of 'Superstition'?

11. Sacha Distel duetted with Brigitte Bardot on a French-language version of which early 1970s Stevie Wonder song?

12. In which year was Wonder involved in a life-threatening car accident?

13. Stevie Wonder celebrated the arrival of his daughter Aisha with which 1976 song, covered the following year by British one-hit wonder David Parton?

14. Which 1987 album featured Michael Jackson guesting on 'Get It'?

15. On which album did Stevie share composer credits with his wife, Syreeta Wright?

NEIL YOUNG

1. Which was Neil Young's so called 'Vocoder album'?

2. In which year did Buffalo Springfield release their first album in the States?

3. Which early Neil Young solo album was mostly recorded in his Topanga Canyon home?

4. What was the second of Young's 'Rust' live albums?

5. Neil Young's *On The Beach* included an end-of-an-era song inspired by his brief association with convicted killer Charles Manson. What was it?

6. Who was the Crazy Horse guitarist who sparred with Young on *Everybody Knows This Is Nowhere*?

7. In which Canadian city was Young born?

8. Young's 'Mr Soul' first appeared on which Buffalo Springfield album?

9. He re-recorded the song – controversially – for which 1980s album?

10. Who is Young's long-time manager?

11. 'Southern Man' first appeared on which Neil Young solo album?

12. Released in 1973, *Time Fades Away* mainly documents a Neil Young tour from which year?

13. Which classic track from Young's 1975 album *Zuma* takes as its subject a 16th-century Spanish conquistador?

14. What was the mid-1980s country album Young recorded with assistance from Waylon Jennings and Willie Nelson?

15. What is Neil Young's only chart-topping solo album in Britain?

ZAPPA / BEEFHEART

1. Only one of these teenage pals from Lancaster, California, kept his real name. What was the birth name of the one who didn't?

2. Which British blues guitarist utters, 'God, it's God, I see God!' at the start of the 1968 Mothers Of Invention album *We're Only In It For The Money*?

3. Beefheart sang guest vocals on which song on Zappa's 1969 *Hot Rats* album?

4. A Mothers Of Invention backing track found its way onto Beefheart's magnum opus, *Trout Mask Replica*. On which song?

5. Zappa protégé Wild Man Fischer sang vocals over a Mothers Of Invention backing track on his 1968 double album *An Evening With Wild Man Fischer*. What was it?

6. Who was Zappa's late-1960s cover artist, famous for sleeve designs such as *Cruising With Ruben And The Jets* and *Burnt Weeny Sandwich*?

7. Jimmy Carl Black, Elliot Ingber, Ian Underwood, Roy Estrada, Art Tripp. Which musician did not cross the divide between Zappa's Mothers Of Invention and Beefheart's Magic Band?

8. Which American actor/folksinger made a guest appearance in Zappa's 1971 film *200 Motels*?

9. Which notable British bass player guested on Zappa's 1973 album *Apostrophe*?

10. Beefheart released two maligned, MOR-inclined albums for Virgin in the mid 1970s. What was the title of the second one?

11. Which punk band covered the Mothers Of Invention's 'Why Don't You Do Me Right'?

12. One of Beefheart's Magic Band members later turned up playing alongside PJ Harvey. Who was he?

13. What was the name of the pro-censorship US campaign group whose activities so enraged Zappa that he testified against them at a Senate hearing in 1985?

14. Which notable television executive has emerged as Zappa and Beefheart's most public champion in recent times?

15. *Over-Nite Sensation* was the title of a 1973 Frank Zappa album. But which US band had a Top 20 US hit single with 'Overnight Sensation'?

BONUS TRACKS

TRACK 01

1. *Before We Were So Rudely Interrupted* was a 1977 reunion album by which leading 1960s act?

2. Who in 1975 was the 'Rhinestone Cowboy'?

3. Which guitarist/singer had joined Wings by the time of *Wild Life* to make the band a four-piece?

4. Who was James Brown's Funky Drummer, and perhaps one of the most sampled musicians in the world?

5. Released in 1966, *The In Sound From Way Out!* was a pioneering electronic music album by which duo?

6. David Vorhaus was the mainstay of which electronic music band famous for the 1969 album *An Electric Storm*?

7. Who wrote *Diary Of A Rock 'n' Roll Star* about his band's 1972 US tour?

8. Why was Sid Vicious arrested in October 1978?

9. Jefferson Airplane, the Flying Burrito Brothers and Santana all played at a large California rock festival on 6 December 1969. By what name is the festival better known?

10. Which influential reggae film premiered in London in September 1972?

11. At which New York club did Television acquire a cult following during 1974 and 1975?

12. What was the name of the band that accompanied k.d. lang on her 1987 major label debut, *Angel With A Lariat*?

13. Which Rod Stewart album topped the album charts in September 1975?

14. What was the title of the 1980 various artists album project that included 51 tracks, each one minute long?

15. What's the title of the 1987 Chuck Berry concert documentary?

TRACK 02

1. What year did *This Is Spinal Tap* arrive in cinemas?

2. Who in 1978 was the 'Werewolves Of London' man?

3. 'Open Your Box' appeared on the flip of which Plastic Ono Band single?

4. Which man-woman pairing reckoned it was 'Too Much Too Little Too Late' in 1978?

5. Who, in 1974, declared *I've Got My Own Album To Do*?

6. Whose well-regarded album is 1985's *This Nation's Saving Grace*?

7. Who, in 1986, was *The Last Of The True Believers*?

8. David Bowie recorded The Beatles' 'Across The Universe' for which album?

9. Which Beatles song did Aerosmith cover successfully in 1978?

10. What early 1980s indie label was dubbed 'The Sound of Young Scotland'?

11. What was George Harrison's first Beatles A-side?

12. Twelve years after his death in 1974, Nick Drake's slim, three-album legacy was augmented by a fourth set of outtakes. What was it called?

13. What was Tim Buckley's last studio album?

14. Who was the man famous for going through Bob Dylan's rubbish?

15. Richie Havens enjoyed a US Top 20 hit with a version of which Beatles song in 1971?

TRACK 03

1. In 1973, Brian Eno and King Crimson guitarist Robert Fripp released an album of experimental music. What was it called?

2. George Jones teamed up with who for the 1980 album *Double Trouble*?

3. Which country singer, in a 1974 hit single, claimed, 'I Can Help'?

4. 1980 saw the release of cult classic *Movies* by which ex-member of Can?

5. Which huge 1970s act started life backing Linda Ronstadt on her 1970 *Silk Purse* album?

6. Which Jagger/Richards song saw release on a Flying Burrito Brothers record before the Stones went public with it?

7. Which band, in 1972, played a series of surprise concerts in universities up and down the country?

8. Who, in 1973, sang of racism in her hit song 'Half-Breed'?

9. Who did the stuttering vocal on Bachman-Turner-Overdrive's 1974 hit 'You Ain't Seen Nothing Yet'?

10. Depeche Mode hail from which Essex new town?

11. Bowie's 'The Jean Genie' and Sweet's 'Blockbuster' both roared up the singles chart at the start of 1973. But which one made it to Number 1?

12. Which glam-affiliated act took their name (via producer Guy Stevens) from a Willard Manus novel?

13. For all their success in Britain, the Bay City Rollers only made it to Number 1 once in the States – with which single?

14. Who on the 1973 hit 'The Joker' made his guitar talk with a slide and wah-wah pedal?

15. What was the hit from Cat Stevens' 1972 album *Catch Bull At Four*?

TRACK 04

1. The Jam's 'Strange Town' was backed by which Jam classic?

2. The Sex Pistols' 'I Wanna Be Me' was coupled with which early punk anthem?

3. To whom was Madness's debut 45, 'The Prince', a tribute?

4. Where did the Ohio Players come from?

5. John Travolta and Olivia Newton-John scored a transatlantic chart-topper in 1978 with 'You're The One That I Want'. But which comedy duo followed up with a British Top 30 version later that year?

6. Which new wave luminary produced the first Specials album?

7. Vi Subversa was singer/guitarist with which radical post-punk act?

8. In December 1978, Sid Vicious attacked the brother of which New York musician with a bottle?

9. 'Keys To Your Heart' was a 1976 pub rock single that featured which future punk notable on vocals and guitar?

10. Who in 1972 duetted with Roberta Flack on 'Where Is The Love'?

11. Which Japan album cover showed David Sylvian eating with chopsticks, a photo of Chairman Mao on the wall behind him?

12. The 1973 album *Baron Von Tolbooth & The Chrome Nun* was credited to Paul Kantner, Grace Slick and which one-time member of Quicksilver Messenger Service?

13. 'Skull Fuck' was the originally desired name for a 1971 double live album by which prolific US band?

14. Who wrote The Who's 'Boris The Spider'?

15. An album of recordings by convicted killer and hippie cult leader Charles Manson was released during his trial at the start of the 1970s. What was it called?

TRACK 05

1. The Beat's rhythm section of Andy Cox and David Steele found themselves back in action as part of which late 1980s pop soul trio?

2. 'Kill The Poor' was which San Francisco-based punk band's ironic solution to society's ills?

3. The cover photo on Gram Parsons' 1973 *GP* album, was taken at which infamous Los Angeles rock hangout?

4. Which electronic trio invited post-punk audiences to 'Do The Mussolini (Headkick)'?

5. Who in 1974 was the *Sweet Exorcist*?

6. 'Let's Build A Car', suggested which gloriously ramshackle post-punk band in 1979?

7. Who shot the photos for the covers of four consecutive Beatles albums?

8. After Big In Japan folded, Liverpool post-punk notable Jane Casey formed which band?

9. Which blues artist was *Going Back To Tennessee* for a 1975 album?

10. Who was 'Looking For The Perfect Beat' in 1982?

11. The Beat debuted in 1979 with a Top 10 version of Smokey Robinson And The Miracles' 'Tears Of A Clown'. But in which year did the original top the British chart?

12. Which legendary Jamaican artist/producer has been known at various times as Chicken Scratch, Little Lee and The Upsetter?

13. Who in 1980 stuck a dole card on the cover of their *Signing Off* album?

14. Who was the producer of the two Joy Division albums?

15. Who produced Siouxsie And The Banshees' *The Scream* and later married singer Kirsty MacColl?

TRACK 06

1. What was the name of Joe Cocker's late 1960s backing band?

2. By which name is Julie Tippetts better known?

3. The subtitle of Scritti Politti's 1984 hit single 'Wood Beez' honoured which US soul legend?

4. Who was brought in to co-produce Duran Duran's 1986 album *Notorious*?

5. Which band did Queen support on tour late in 1973?

6. Annie Lennox wore a leather eye mask on the cover of which Eurythmics album?

7. Olivia Newton-John's 1971 breakthrough single was 'If Not For You'. Who wrote it?

8. Which noted artist, later regarded as providing the visual inspiration for Ridley Scott's *Alien*, designed the cover for ELP's *Brain Salad Surgery*?

9. Who was the big man behind the Love Unlimited Orchestra?

10. Big Brother & The Holding Company's *Cheap Thrills* album from 1968 sported artwork by which acid-era graphic artist?

11. In what year did Art Garfunkel hit with 'Bright Eyes'?

12. Which Human League album cover featured babies being danced over?

13. Who, in 1973, asked, 'Will It Go Round In Circles'?

14. Accompanying the Buzzcocks on their late 1979 tour were which up-and-coming band also from Manchester?

15. What is the name given to that army of happy tapers who followed the Grateful Dead everywhere?

TRACK 07

1. Robert Palmer's vocal sparring partner in early 1970s good-time rock 'n' roll band Vinegar Joe also went on to enjoy a hugely successful solo career. Who was she?

2. What was the record label formed by Ringo in the mid 1970s?

3. A 1966 'funny' by someone calling himself Napoleon XIV fell foul of some radio programmers in the States, who felt it made light of mental health issues. What was it called?

4. Who did not audition for The Monkees? a) Davy Jones b) Stephen Stills c) Charles Manson

5. Better known as the godfather of Eurodisco, via his work with Donna Summer, Giorgio Moroder tasted success as early as 1972 by writing a crossover bubblegum/glam Number 1 hit. What was it?

6. The Rainbow Theatre was probably London's most prominent rock venue during the 1970s. It also hosted numerous 1960s package tours under an earlier name. Which was?

7. The Pogues' 1985 album *Rum, Sodomy & The Lash* featured a cover adapted from which early 19th-century painting by Gericault?

8. What is Boy George's real name?

9. Björk came to prominence in her native Iceland in 1976 with a cover of which contemporary disco hit?

10. Prior to breaking through in 1975 with 'All By Myself', Eric Carmen led which Beatles-inspired band?

11. In which year did Cher and Sonny Bono split up?

12. Which huge 1970s band released the much-ignored album *Heroes Are Hard To Find* in 1974?

13. What was Ginger Baker's first post-Blind Faith band?

14. What was the full title of the well-dressed Beatles compilation from 1966 that rounded up many of the band's early singles?

15. 1987's *Locust Abortion Technician* was an extraordinary album from which bunch of Texas-based miscreants?

TRACK 08

1. After his death in 1977, some pre-fame recordings by Marc Bolan were given a contemporary rock-band feel and stuck out on an album. What was it called?

2. Which left-field electronic band hit the dancefloor running with *The Crackdown*, their 1983 debut for Virgin Records?

3. Nick Cave And The Bad Seeds' *Kicking Against The Pricks* album title was potentially inspired by a book and/or a writer. Name either.

4. After the demise of Family, singer Roger Chapman and Charlie Whitney released one album. Title?

5. What does the band acronym GTOs stand for?

6. Jacqui McShee sang with which distinguished folk-rock act?

7. Who, in 1979, sang despairingly of 'Typical Girls'?

8. Gong mainman Daevid Allen had previously been a member of which great British psychedelic band?

9. Who moaned and sighed her way through the innuendo-packed 'Down Deep Inside' single from 1977?

10. Soft Cell had a hit in 1982 with which Judy Street Northern Soul original?

11. Which 1984 12" 23 Skidoo single anticipated the electro-funk big beat sound exemplified by the Chemical Brothers a decade later?

12. Initial copies of which Wire album came with a free EP?

13. Which punk band celebrated 'The Day The World Turned Day-Glo'?

14. What was the title of the 1977 triple-disc Neil Young retrospective?

15. Which mostly live Frank Zappa set from 1975 also included notable contributions from Captain Beefheart?

TRACK 09

1.   Which English actress/singer found herself in a Montreal hotel room in June 1969 and contributing to John and Yoko's anti-war single, 'Give Peace A Chance'?

2.   Who was Fairport Convention's fiddle player?

3.   The New Temple Missionary Baptist Church in Los Angeles was the venue for an acclaimed Aretha Franklin recording, captured on which 1972 album?

4.   Where, in July 1973, did David Bowie make his retirement speech, effectively disbanding the Spiders From Mars?

5.   Who was Dr Funkenstein?

6.   What did Michael Jackson do for the first time at Motown's 25th-anniversary show in Pasadena, California, in 1983?

7.   Ex-Generation X bassist Tony James was the band's driving force, but who was Sigue Sigue Sputnik's flamboyant frontman?

8.   Which founder member of Cabaret Voltaire has since become a respected sound recordist, specifically for wildlife documentaries?

9.   Who in 1978 had an early independent hit with 'Being Boiled'?

10. Who, in 1981, declared himself a Homosapien?

11. Who, in 1975, advised, 'Listen To What The Man Said'?

12. Steely Dan took their name from a sex toy in a novel by which Beat writer?

13. George Harrison's 'Old Brown Shoe' appeared on the B-side of which Beatles single?

14. Who was the muscle behind US hardcore band Big Black, and a key player in toughening up the sound of rock during grunge and beyond?

15. Which band, in 1983, were *Perverted By Language*?

TRACK 10

1. Santana's triple album epic, recorded live at the Budokan in 1973, was an expensive – and elaborately designed – import release in 1975. What was it called?

2. Which punk band from the North East of England debuted with a single called 'Don't Dictate'?

3. A John Peel-backed underground two-piece, Machine Head, had a couple of surprise hits in 1973. Name one of them.

4. Which of the Allman Brothers' drummers possessed a classic rock 'n' roll name?

5. 'Jackie Wilson Said (I'm In Heaven When You Smile)' appeared on which Van Morrison album?

6. Who scored a minor British hit single in 1973 with the retro-sounding 'I Saw The Light'?

7. Whose 1975 single 'Rosalie' was a cover of a Bob Seger song?

8. Which US radio rockers struck big with 'More Than A Feeling'?

9. Who was Liz Fraser's 'Cocteau Twin'?

10. No longer fronted by ex-Animals singer Eric Burdon, War re-emerged in 1972 with which US chart-topping album?

11. Which Afrobeat pioneer took British drum legend Ginger Baker under his wing in the early 1970s?

12. *Flip Your Wig* was the last Hüsker Dü album to appear on which California-based independent label?

13. 'Barbarism Begins At Home' was a declaration made by which band?

14. According to the 1985 Starship hit, 'We Built This City On...' a) Sex and alcohol b) Rock 'n' roll c) A gangster's moll

15. In what year did singing sticksman Phil Collins suggest *No Jacket Required*?

THE ANSWERS

SIDE A

ALIASES

1. Bernard Jewry

2. Stuart Goddard

3. Paul Hewson

4. Vincent Furnier

5. William Broad

6. Reg Dwight

7. Marvin (Lee) Aday – which he changed to Michael Lee Aday in 2001

8. Roberta Anderson

9. James Osterberg

10. Lewis Allan Reed

11. Mary O'Brien

12. Sylvester Stewart

13. John Mellor

14. Anna Mae Bullock

15. Barry Eugene Carter

ALL ABOUT THE USA

1. The Skids

2. Human League

3. David Bowie

4. The Clash

5. James Brown

6. Kim Wilde

7. Jefferson Airplane

8. Ian Hunter

9. Don McLean

10. The Guess Who

11. Supertramp

12. The Work

13. The Doors

14. David Lee Roth

15. The Beach Boys

ANIMALS

1. Pink Floyd

2. Michael Jackson

3. The Beatles

4. Curved Air

5. Country Joe McDonald

6. Cat Stevens

7. America

8. Tyrannosaurus Rex

9. Frank Zappa

10. Grateful Dead

11. Pink Floyd

12. The Doors (original: John Lee Hooker)

13. Joni Mitchell or Country Joe McDonald

14. Jefferson Airplane

15. Art Bears

BANNED RECORDS

1. Brigitte Bardot

2. W.A.S.P.

3. 'Let's spend some time together'

4. 1969

5. 'Urban Guerilla'

6. *Yesterday And Today*

7. 'Lola' by The Kinks

8. 'God Save The Queen' by the Sex Pistols

9. 'Walk On The Wild Side'

10. 'Too Drunk To Fuck'

11. 1968

12. '(We Don't Need This) Fascist Groove Thang'

13. *Straight Outta Compton*

14. Melanie

15. Derek and Clive

BEATLES COVERS

1. 'Martha My Dear'

2. 'Tomorrow Never Knows'

3. 'Help!'

4. 'All You Need Is Love'

5. 'Ticket To Ride'

6. Del Shannon

7. Richie Havens

8. 'The Fool On The Hill'

9. 'In My Life'

10. 'Tomorrow Never Knows'

11. 'Come Together'

12. Stevie Wonder

13. Joe Cocker

14. 'Eleanor Rigby'

15. 'Lucy In The Sky With Diamonds'

CHARITY RECORDS

1. Ronnie Lane

2. Amnesty International

3. Bob Dylan

4. Ravi Shankar

5. Save The Children

6. 'That's What Friends Are For'

7. John Lennon

8. Quincy Jones

9. Willie Nelson

10. The *Conspiracy Of Hope* tour

11. Stevie Wonder

12. Neil Young

13. Robert Stigwood

14. Jethro Tull

15. 'Last Christmas'

CHRISTMAS CRACKERS

1. David Bowie

2. Wham!

3. Shakin' Stevens

4. The Waitresses

5. Slade

6. Jethro Tull

7. Kate Bush

8. Paul McCartney

9. The Pogues

10. Mike Oldfield

11. John & Yoko / Plastic Ono Band

12. Steeleye Span

13. Mud

14. Run-DMC

15. The Dickies

CLASSIC ALBUM COVERS

1. Roger Dean

2. Barney Bubbles

3. Robert Frank

4. Cat Stevens

5. Pennie Smith

6. Ray Lowry

7. Joni Mitchell

8. Guy Peellaert

9. Mick Rock

10. Kelly / Mouse

11. Hipgnosis / Storm Thorgerson

12. Roberta Bayley

13. Craig Braun

14. Bryan Ferry

15. Roger Dean

CLASSIC DEBUTS

1.   1975

2.   1970

3.   1977

4.   1969

5.   1968

6.   1979

7.   1987

8.   1978

9.   1972

10. 1987

11. 1984

12. 1970

13. 1979

14. 1970

15. 1976

CLASSIC LIVE ALBUMS

1. MC5

2. The Who

3. Hawkwind

4. Jefferson Airplane

5. Miles Davis

6. Grateful Dead

7. Elvis Presley

8. Funkadelic

9. Melanie

10. Mahavishnu Orchestra

11. Various Artists

12. Humble Pie

13. Frank Zappa & The Mothers

14. Tim Buckley

15. The Rolling Stones

CLASSICAL GAS

1. Mussorgsky

2. *Swan Lake*

3. 'Hall Of The Mountain King'

4. *Fans*

5. 'Also Sprach Zarathustra'

6. Albinoni

7. Love Sculpture

8. Vivaldi

9. Aaron Copland's 'Fanfare For The Common Man'

10. Deep Purple

11. Brian Eno

12. '10538 Overture'

13. Holst's *The Planets*

14. 'Bouree'

15. 'Jupiter'

COLLABORATIONS

1. *St Valentine's Day Massacre*

2. *(No Pussyfooting)*

3. *Silly Sisters*

4. *Rough Mix*

5. Dionne Warwick

6. Snatch

7. Curtis Knight

8. Afrika Bambaataa

9. *Illuminations*

10. The Jeff Beck Group

11. Eddie Kendricks

12. George Harrison

13. Lydia Lunch

14. Eddie Murphy

15. Bananarama

COLOURS

1. *Lodger*

2. Blue Weaver

3. 1982

4. New Order

5. Alan White

6. Roy Orbison

7. Jeff Beck

8. 1970

9. Mud

10. *My Aim Is True*

11. 'Gypsy Queen'

12. 1982

13. Priscilla White

14. Yellow

15. Pink Anderson

CONCEPT ALBUMS

1. Jeff Wayne

2. *Preservation Act 1*

3. *Histoire De Melody Nelson*

4. *Tales From Topographic Oceans*

5. *Nineteen Eighty-Four*

6. *Eldorado*

7. Roger Glover

8. *Welcome To My Nightmare*

9. Mike Nesmith

10. *That's Life*

11. Pete Townshend

12. The Pretty Things

13. *Consequences*

14. Gentle Giant

15. Rick Wakeman

CONNECTIONS

1. *Willy And The Poor Boys* was a 1969 Creedence Clearwater Revival album; *Willie & The Poor Boys* was a 1985 solo album by Bill Wyman

2. Roy Wood formed ELO with Jeff Lynne, then quit to form Wizzard

3. Costello had a long on-off relationship with Tyler's mother, model Bebe Buell

4. They were both recorded at Musicland Studios in Munich

5. They have both covered Doors songs

6. Sleeve designer Barney Bubbles

7. Almond's Soft Cell had an enormous hit with 'Tainted Love', originally a Northern Soul classic by Bolan's partner Gloria Jones

8. Gaye's 'Baby Don't You Do It' was covered by both bands

9. They were both in mid-1960s beat combo Wainwright's Gentlemen

10. The same classic shot from 1927 of a tornado graced Deep Purple's *Stormbringer* and the Banshees' *Tinderbox* albums

11. Mae Axton co-wrote the Elvis Presley hit, while her son Hoyt wrote 'Joy To The World'. And both were US Number 1 hits

12. Bon Jovi's second cousin Tony Bongiovi worked with producer Alan Douglas on some posthumous Jimi Hendrix recordings

13. 'Dog Eat Dog' was a single for Adam And The Ants and the title of a Joni Mitchell album

14. They both released albums titled *Phantasmagoria*

15. Bob Johnston

COVER VERSIONS

1. Frankie Goes To Hollywood

2. 'Alabama Song'

3. Melanie

4. 'God Only Knows'

5. 1990

6. Manfred Mann's Earth Band

7. Labelle

8. This Mortal Coil

9. 'A Message To You, Rudy'

10. Robert Wyatt

11. 1987

12. Dolly Parton

13. Harold Melvin & The Blue Notes

14. Al Green

15. Ken Boothe

A DATE WITH...

1.   January 1969

2.   December 1976

3.   October 1975

4.   December 1985

5.   August 1969

6.   August 1981

7.   January 1973

8.   August 1982

9.   April 1970

10. February 1980

11. July 1985

12. January 1972

13. October 1982

14. July 1977

15. August 1977

DEAD FAMOUS

1. Florence Ballard

2. Pete Farndon

3. Tommy Bolin

4. The Strawbs

5. Tim Hardin

6. John Denver

7. The Rossington-Collins Band

8. Brian Jones

9. Todd Haynes

10. The Dead Boys

11. 1983

12. Malcolm Owen

13. Terry Kath

14. Ron McKernan

15. Al Wilson

DISCO SUCKS

1. Jacques Morali

2. Bronski Beat

3. 'Summer Night City'

4. Eric Clapton

5. Mike Chapman

6. 'That's The Way (I Like It)'

7. *Destiny*

8. Both were produced by Biddu

9. 'Hold Back The Night'

10. *Thank God It's Friday*

11. Barry White

12. 'Boogie Nights'

13. 'Le Freak'

14. 'Dancin' Fool'

15. Björk

DON'T BE DAFT: 15 NOVELTY SONGS

1. Black Lace
2. Ray Stevens
3. Lieutenant Pigeon
4. 'Weird Al' Yankovic
5. Rick Dees And His Cast Of Idiots
6. Keith Harris & Orville
7. The Pipkins
8. Joe Dolce
9. Shag
10. Spitting Image
11. Chuck Berry
12. Hylda Baker & Arthur Mullard
13. David Bowie
14. The Tweets
15. Carl Douglas

EARLIER BANDS / BAND NAMES

1. 'The Nazz Are Blue'

2. Creedence Clearwater Revival

3. *Maybe Tomorrow*

4. The Frantic Elevators

5. None

6. ABC

7. Southern Death Cult

8. The Police

9. Simple Minds

10. The Boys Next Door

11. 'That'll Be The Day'

12. Genesis

13. Simon and Garfunkel

14. (Bob Marley and) The Wailers

15. Chic

EASY LISTENING: SLEEPING WITH THE ENEMY

1. The Peter Thomas Sound Orchestra

2. Brandy

3. James Last

4. Herman's Hermits

5. *Lost Horizon*

6. Claudine Longet

7. A&M

8. Demis Roussos

9. The Beat

10. Jean-Jacques Perrey

11. Martin Denny

12. 'Goodbye To Love'

13. The Johnny Mann Singers

14. Ted Nugent

15. Burt Bacharach and Hal David

EIGHTIES POP

1. 'The Power Of Love'

2. 1983

3. *Vive Le Rock*

4. Jennifer Rush

5. Mark Knopfler

6. Bread

7. Billy Bragg

8. *Speak & Spell*

9. Mark Hollis

10. Stephen Duffy

11. Switzerland

12. Thomas Dolby

13. 'Let's Make Lots Of Money'

14. Dave Ball

15. *Architecture And Morality*

EPICS

1. 'Supper's Ready'
2. *Brain Salad Surgery*
3. Traffic
4. *Hot Buttered Soul*
5. *Pawn Hearts*
6. 'Dazed And Confused'
7. *Meddle*
8. '2112'
9. *A Passion Play*
10. Colosseum
11. Leslie West
12. *Third*
13. 'Love To Love You Baby'
14. 22 minutes
15. Ian Anderson

FAR-OUT ACID ROCK

1. Jefferson Airplane

2. Jimi Hendrix Experience

3. Country Joe & The Fish

4. The Pink Floyd

5. Cream

6. The Who

7. Traffic

8. Quicksilver Messenger Service

9. The Beatles

10. The Chambers Brothers

11. Captain Beefheart & His Magic Band

12. Big Brother & The Holding Company

13. The Rolling Stones

14. The Doors

15. Love

FESTIVALS

1. Sweet

2. 1982

3. Bickershaw Festival

4. 1988

5. Wattstax

6. Sid Vicious

7. The Elephant Fayre

8. Watkins Glen

9. 1985

10. 1968

11. Malcolm McLaren

12. Led Zeppelin

13. 1971

14. The Toronto Rock 'n' Roll Revival

15. 1980

FIFTH BEATLE

1. Billy Preston

2. Neil Aspinall

3. Stuart Sutcliffe

4. George Martin

5. Jeff Lynne

6. Brian Epstein

7. Pete Best

8. John Peel

9. Eric Clapton

10. Yoko Ono

11. Mal Evans

12. Barry Miles

13. Allen Klein

14. Dick James

15. Derek Taylor

FILM CONNECTION / SCREEN DREAMS

1. Russ Meyer

2. Peter Wyngarde

3. Richard Harris

4. Faye Dunaway

5. Hayley Mills

6. *Straight to Hell*

7. 'What's Love Got To Do With It'

8. *Return To Waterloo*

9. 'Pretty In Pink'

10. Marilyn Monroe

11. *Flesh*

12. Martin Kemp

13. Jon Voight

14. Mahalia Jackson

15. *The Breakfast Club*

FILMS IN SONG

1. Bette Davis (in 'Bette Davis Eyes')

2. Suzanne Vega

3. Dirk Bogarde

4. Humphrey Bogart

5. Haysi Fantayzee

6. Bananarama

7. Alice Cooper

8. David Bowie

9. Pere Ubu

10. Gregory Peck

11. François Truffaut

12. *Angels with Dirty Faces*

13. Tuxedomoon

14. 'Wild Is The Wind'

15. 'The Seventh Seal'

GLAM

1. Jobriath

2. Saxon

3. Mud

4. 'What's Your Name' / 'Good Grief Christina'

5. 'Dear Elaine'

6. 'How Does It Feel'

7. *Godspell*

8. Nicky Chinn and Mike Chapman

9. Detroit

10. Mike Leander

11. 'Ballroom Blitz'

12. Mott The Hoople

13. 'Angel Face'

14. Ron

15. Peter Noone

GLAM RACKET

1. T. Rex

2. Mott The Hoople

3. Wizzard

4. Eno

5. Sweet

6. David Bowie

7. New York Dolls

8. Gary Glitter

9. David Essex

10. Suzi Quatro

11. The Faces

12. Slade

13. Alice Cooper

14. Sparks

15. Roxy Music

GOING IT ALONE

1. Steve Hillage (from Gong)

2. Lowell George (from Little Feat)

3. Mick Jagger (from the Rolling Stones)

4. Diana Ross (from The Supremes)

5. Steve Winwood (from Traffic)

6. Elkie Brooks (from Vinegar Joe)

7. Curtis Mayfield (from The Impressions)

8. Bob Geldof (from The Boomtown Rats)

9. David Coverdale (from Deep Purple)

10. Michael Jackson (from the Jackson 5)

11. Annie Haslam (from Renaissance)

12. Jack Bruce (from Cream)

13. Julian Cope (from the Teardrop Explodes)

14. Robert Fripp (from King Crimson)

15. David Ruffin (from The Temptations)

GREAT LABELS

1. Stax

2. Blanco Y Negro

3. Bearsville

4. Island

5. Def Jam

6. Track

7. Rough Trade

8. ZTT

9. Motown

10. Elektra

11. Blast First

12. Trojan

13. Stiff

14. 4AD

15. SST

GUESTS

1. Scarlet Rivera

2. Paul McCartney

3. *Rain Dogs*

4. *You're Under Arrest*

5. Vincent Crane

6. Syd Barrett

7. Marc Bolan

8. Mick Jagger

9. Rick Wakeman

10. Stevie Wonder

11. Material

12. Phil Collins

13. Peter Gabriel

14. Neneh Cherry

15. Buddy Miles

GUITARISTS

1. Johnny Thunders

2. Joe Walsh

3. John McLaughlin

4. Jeff Beck

5. 'Eruption'

6. David Knopfler

7. *Star Fleet Project*

8. Eddie Hazel

9. Alan Douglas

10. Fred Frith

11. Tomorrow

12. *Bridge Of Sighs*

13. Steve Cropper

14. Florida

15. Quiet Sun

HARD ROCK AND METAL

1. Neal Kay

2. Grand Funk Railroad

3. 'Here I Go Again'

4. Kirk Hammett

5. Blue Cheer

6. Bass

7. *Electric*

8. *Master Of Puppets*

9. Barry Hay

10. Steppenwolf

11. Jim Dandy

12. *Live?!*@ Like A Suicide*

13. *Toys In The Attic*

14. Jim Steinman

15. *Sounds*

HARD-UP HEROES

1. 'In A Broken Dream'

2. Poly Styrene

3. Elton John

4. Jimi Hendrix

5. Arthur Lee

6. Radiohead

7. Little Boy Blue & The Blue Boys

8. The Great Society

9. Suzi Quatro

10. Decca

11. Bob Dylan

12. Slade

13. U2

14. Bob Seger

15. Marc Bolan

HE'S THE BOSS – AND SO IS SHE!

1. The Beatles

2. Sex Pistols

3. Led Zeppelin

4. Joy Division / New Order

5. The Clash

6. Ozzy Osbourne

7. The Move

8. The Rolling Stones

9. David Bowie

10. Bee Gees / Eric Clapton

11. Iron Maiden

12. Genesis

13. Frank Zappa

14. Pink Floyd

15. Jimi Hendrix / Slade

HIP HOP

1. Chuck D

2. De La Soul

3. *Radio*

4. Ice-T

5. Russell Simmons

6. Terminator X

7. Afrika Bambaataa

8. Melle Mel

9. Boogie Down Productions

10. 1984

11. The Bronx

12. Keith LeBlanc

13. Eric B. & Rakim

14. 1977

15. 'No Sleep Till Brooklyn'

HOBBIES

1. Alice Cooper

2. Mick Jagger

3. Nick Mason

4. Kenney Jones

5. Slash

6. Lemmy

7. Dave Murray

8. Bruce Dickinson

9. Brian May

10. Rod Stewart

11. Charlie Watts

12. Aretha Franklin

13. Jeff Beck

14. Grandmaster Flash

15. Cherie Currie

JAZZ ROCK

1. *Apocalypse*

2. *Live At Leeds*

3. *Head Hunters*

4. George Benson

5. Mahavishnu Orchestra

6. Keith Jarrett

7. Santana

8. Stanley Clarke

9. Didier Malherbe

10. 1970

11. Frank Zappa

12. Graham Bond

13. Lifetime

14. Dave Holland

15. Larry Coryell

KRAUTROCK

1. *Dance Of The Lemmings*

2. Can singer Damo Suzuki (on 'I Am Damo Suzuki')

3. *Krautrocksampler*

4. Faust

5. Tangerine Dream

6. 'Da Da Da'

7. Big Black

8. Malcolm Mooney

9. Renate Knaup

10. *Faust IV*

11. Neu!

12. Düsseldorf

13. Werner Herzog

14. Conny Plank

15. Traffic

LABEL ASSOCIATIONS

1. RCA

2. Motown

3. Philips

4. Capitol

5. Island

6. Arista

7. Harvest

8. Elektra

9. Sire

10. 2-Tone

11. Chess

12. A&M

13. Chrysalis

14. EMI

15. United Artists

LOVE MUSIC

1. The Damned

2. Golden Earring

3. Rose Royce

4. Kim Wilde

5. Bob Marley & The Wailers

6. O'Jays

7. Public Image Ltd (PiL)

8. Barry White

9. Ten Years After

10. The Cure

11. Depeche Mode

12. Fleetwood Mac

13. B-52's

14. Richard Hell & The Voidoids

15. Tom Tom Club

MATCH THE SINGER AND THE BAND

1. Roxy Music

2. Jethro Tull

3. Raspberries

4. Cameo

5. Hot Chocolate

6. Pere Ubu

7. Thin Lizzy

8. The Commodores

9. Orange Juice

10. Rush

11. Poison

12. Supertramp

13. The Selecter

14. The Damned

15. Talking Heads

MISSING WORDS: ALBUM TITLES

1. *Torpedoes*
2. *Life*
3. *Head*
4. *Eagle*
5. *World*
6. *Ass*
7. *Hassle*
8. *Astral*
9. *Music*
10. *Chicken*
11. *Loaded*
12. *Shop*
13. *Psyche*
14. *Poseidon*
15. *Mothership*

MISSING WORDS: BAND NAMES

1. Schwarz

2. Altered

3. Teardrop

4. Sensational

5. Whole

6. Nine

7. Trash

8. Link Wray

9. Captain

10. Brand

11. Chance

12. Head

13. Street

14. Blackhearts

15. B

MISSING WORDS: SONG TITLES

1. Hills

2. Jezebel

3. Hurricane

4. Sleazy

5. Spurts

6. Piano

7. 21

8. Fear

9. Night

10. Luv

11. Dustpipe

12. Hurt

13. Dead

14. Balance

15. Home

MONTHS

1. Pilot

2. Queen Elizabeth Hall

3. Robert Wyatt

4. July

5. *Hot August Night*

6. Earth, Wind & Fire

7. October

8. The Jesus And Mary Chain

9. 'Remember'

10. *The Wild, The Innocent & The E Street Shuffle*

11. Iron Maiden

12. Bee Gees

13. Al Stewart

14. *Four Sail*

15. Kurt Weill

NEW WAVE

1. Larry Wallis

2. Ultravox!

3. Nick Lowe

4. *The Fine Art Of Surfacing*

5. Ray Davies

6. John Shuttleworth

7. The Monks

8. Frantic Elevators

9. Martin Luther King Jr

10. Rick Buckler

11. Graham Parker And The Rumour

12. Thin Lizzy

13. 'My Perfect Cousin'

14. Bill Nelson

15. Akron

NEW WAVE, OLD WAVE

1. Randy & The Rainbows

2. Dusty Springfield

3. Righteous Brothers

4. Smokey Robinson & The Miracles

5. The Strangeloves

6. Tommy James & The Shondells

7. The Yardbirds

8. Al Green

9. Tommy James & The Shondells

10. Barrett Strong

11. Reparata And The Delrons

12. Sly And The Family Stone

13. The Rolling Stones

14. The Kinks

15. The Moody Blues

NUMBER 2s

1. 1976
2. 1970
3. 1979
4. 1984
5. 1983
6. 1982
7. 1982
8. 1983
9. 1979
10. 1975
11. 1973
12. 1972
13. 1976
14. 1980
15. 1986

NUMBERS

1. Boomtown Rats
2. Kim Weston
3. Led Zeppelin
4. David Bowie
5. Iron Maiden
6. Lene Lovich
7. The Jags
8. 'Virginia Plain'
9. Soft Cell
10. Styx
11. Top 10
12. 1973
13. Lionel Richie
14. Public Enemy
15. Steely Dan

THE OFFSPRING

1. Mick Jagger

2. China

3. 'Too Late For Goodbyes'

4. Gary Lucas

5. Nona Gaye

6. Jakob Dylan

7. Mary McCartney

8. Moon Unit Zappa

9. Duncan Jones

10. 'Sketches For My Sweetheart The Drunk'

11. 'The First Time Ever I Saw Your Face'

12. Nick Cave

13. Bebe Buell

14. Don Arden

15. Anna

OUT OF THE BLUE: 15 UNLIKELY HIT SINGLES

1. Laurie Anderson

2. Donna Summer

3. Siouxsie And The Banshees

4. Focus

5. Isaac Hayes

6. Lieutenant Pigeon

7. PiL

8. Herbie Hancock

9. Hawkwind

10. Flying Lizards

11. David Essex

12. The B-52's

13. Lene Lovich

14. Paul Hardcastle

15. Kraftwerk

PARTNERS

1. Chrissie Hynde
2. Peter Sellers
3. Ben Watt
4. Anna Gordy
5. 52
6. Kris Kristofferson
7. Amanda Donohoe
8. Janis Joplin
9. Syreeta Wright
10. Angie Bowie
11. Carrie Snodgress
12. John Dunbar
13. 1968
14. Pamela Courson
15. Budgie

PLACES

1. Gerry Rafferty

2. Duran Duran

3. The Doors

4. Pet Shop Boys

5. Gladys Knight & The Pips

6. Ultravox

7. David Bowie

8. Peter Gabriel

9. The Clash

10. Scott Walker

11. Led Zeppelin

12. Ralph McTell

13. 10cc

14. Martha & The Muffins

15. Elvis Costello

POLITICS

1. Angelic Upstarts

2. The Beat

3. George Jackson

4. Queen

5. Michael Buerk

6. The Pop Group

7. Coventry

8. Paul and Linda McCartney

9. 1972

10. The Beach Boys

11. 1979

12. Au Pairs

13. Dead Kennedys

14. Abbie Hoffman

15. Chuck D

POST-PUNK

1. Futurama

2. Rough Trade

3. A Dada club in First World War Zurich

4. The Passage

5. Edouard Manet

6. *Perverted By Language*

7. Albert Camus (*The Outsider*)

8. Throbbing Gristle

9. Dennis 'Blackbeard' Bovell

10. *United States Live*

11. The Pop Group

12. Liliput

13. Gang Of Four

14. Spizzenergi

15. Lemon Kittens

PRE-PUNK

1. Todd Rundgren

2. The Neon Boys

3. Leee Black Childers

4. Billy Murcia

5. *Country, Blue Grass, Blues and Other Music for Uplifting Gourmandizers*

6. Flamin' Groovies

7. *Neu! '75*

8. Let It Rock

9. *Down By The Jetty*

10. Lenny Kaye

11. Pink Fairies

12. *Transformer*

13. The Elgin

14. Grande Ballroom

15. The Troggs

PRESLEY 70S

1. Brenda Lee

2. Judy Collins

3. Engelbert Humperdinck

4. Mickey Newbury

5. Don McLean

6. *Man of La Mancha*

7. Gordon Lightfoot

8. 'I'm So Lonesome I Could Cry'

9. 'Burning Love'

10. John Fogerty

11. 'Until It's Time For You To Go'

12. Kris Kristofferson

13. *Elvis Country*

14. Marty Robbins

15. Perry Como

PRODUCERS

1. Phil Spector

2. Jac Holzman

3. Mayo Thompson

4. Sandy Pearlman

5. Lee Perry

6. Shania Twain

7. Lou Adler

8. *Beggars Banquet*

9. Chris Thomas

10. David Bowie and Mick Ronson

11. Todd Rundgren

12. Chris Blackwell

13. Willie Mitchell

14. George Clinton

15. Teo Macero

PROG

1. Tony Kaye

2. *Journey*

3. A loud gong

4. *Angels Egg*

5. Geoff Downes

6. Wrote a song inspired by British actress Susan Penhaligon

7. Simon Dupree & The Big Sound

8. *Still*

9. Aphrodite's Child

10. *End Of An Ear*

11. Atomic Rooster

12. Thijs van Leer

13. Empire Pool, Wembley

14. 'Owner Of A Lonely Heart'

15. Pink Floyd

PROG ROCK ON 45

1. Genesis

2. Rare Bird

3. Van Der Graaf Generator

4. Curved Air

5. The Moody Blues

6. Yes

7. Emerson, Lake & Palmer

8. Jethro Tull

9. Focus

10. Argent

11. Manfred Mann's Earthband

12. Atomic Rooster

13. Family

14. PFM

15. Procol Harum

PUNK

1. David Bowie

2. *Sniffin' Glue… And Other Rock 'n' Roll Habits…*

3. *Road To Ruin*

4. Acme Attractions

5. Eric's

6. '(I'm) Stranded'

7. The Lurkers

8. Throbbing Gristle

9. The Vibrators

10. Toyah

11. Buzzcocks

12. Poly Styrene

13. 'Gary Gilmore's Eyes'

14. Ramones

15. Brian James

PUNK ON FIRE

1. The Clash

2. The Ruts

3. Sex Pistols

4. Sham 69

5. X-Ray Spex

6. The Slits

7. Alternative TV

8. Siouxsie & The Banshees

9. The Mekons

10. Magazine

11. The Stranglers

12. Subway Sect

13. Pere Ubu

14. The Damned

15. The Adverts

RADIO

1. *The Perfumed Garden*

2. Dave Lee Travis

3. Radio Caroline

4. September 1967

5. 'Calling Occupants Of Interplanetary Craft'

6. Elvis Costello & The Attractions

7. Matthew Bannister

8. Alan Freeman

9. 'W.O.L.D.'

10. John Walters

11. Kenny Everett

12. Tommy Vance

13. Arnold

14. Marc Riley And The Creepers

15. Mike Read

REGGAE

1. (Toots And) The Maytals
2. Neil Diamond
3. Althea And Donna
4. Dennis 'Blackbeard' Bovell
5. Musical Youth
6. Culture
7. Augustus Pablo
8. Steel Pulse
9. Burning Spear
10. Dennis Brown
11. *Marcus Garvey*
12. Gregory Isaacs
13. Linton Kwesi Johnson
14. Smiley Culture
15. Prince Far I

REVIVE 45

1.   The Shangri-Las

2.   Small Faces

3.   David Bowie

4.   Neil Sedaka

5.   The Chiffons

6.   B. Bumble & The Stingers

7.   Mary Wells

8.   Little Eva

9.   Jackie Wilson

10. Jeff Beck

11. Roy C

12. The Moody Blues

13. The Goons

14. Bobby 'Boris' Pickett And The Crypt-Kickers

15. David Bowie

THE ROCK INVASION

1. Jethro Tull

2. Chicago

3. Canned Heat

4. Frijid Pink

5. The Move

6. Fleetwood Mac

7. Free

8. Family

9. Deep Purple

10. Black Sabbath

11. The Jimi Hendrix Experience

12. C.C.S.

13. East Of Eden

14. Atomic Rooster

15. Curved Air

ROCK 'N' ROLL

1. 'Rumble'

2. Dion

3. The Art Of Noise

4. Rick Nelson

5. Billy Fury

6. Ricky Wilde

7. Jerry Lee Lewis

8. The Drifters

9. Stray Cats

10. 1981

11. 'Reelin' And Rockin''

12. They had long hair

13. Ian Dury

14. *Roots: John Lennon Sings The Great Rock & Roll Hits*

15. 'Summertime Blues'

SESSION MEN

1. Nicky Hopkins

2. Motown

3. Tony Levin

4. Herbie Flowers

5. Ray Cooper

6. Carole Kaye

7. Paul McCartney

8. Andy Newmark

9. Dennis Davis

10. James Jamerson

11. Waddy Wachtel

12. Sheila E

13. Larry Knechtel

14. John Paul Jones

15. Head Hands & Feet

SINGER-SONGWRITERS

1. Laura Nyro

2. *Tapestry* (by Carole King)

3. 'A World Without Love' was a hit for Peter & Gordon, Peter being Peter Asher, future manager/producer of James Taylor

4. David Ackles

5. *Tess of the d'Urbervilles*

6. Kevin Coyne

7. Bridget St. John

8. *Annie Hall*

9. *Cosmic Wheels*

10. Bill Fay

11. Suzanne Vega

12. Fred Neil

13. Paul Simon

14. The Wurzels

15. Christy Moore

SONGS ABOUT STARS AND STARDOM

1. David Essex

2. Deep Purple

3. The Rolling Stones

4. David Bowie

5. Sly And The Family Stone

6. Rose Royce

7. Sonic Youth

8. Stevie Wonder

9. Judas Priest

10. The Passions

11. Grateful Dead

12. Bad Company

13. The Carpenters

14. Buggles

15. The Firm

SONGS ABOUT TRAVEL

1. Tom Robinson Band

2. Canned Heat

3. The O'Jays

4. Paul and Linda McCartney

5. Bruce Springsteen

6. Bee Gees

7. The Floaters

8. Pink Floyd

9. Deep Purple

10. Buzzcocks

11. Eagles

12. The Supremes

13. The Temptations

14. Spandau Ballet

15. The Jimi Hendrix Experience

SOUL

1. 'Me And Mrs Jones'

2. Love Unlimited

3. Ernie Isley

4. 'Drift Away'

5. The Sound of Philadelphia

6. Gil Scott-Heron

7. Aretha Franklin

8. 'Tell Me Something Good'

9. Willie Mitchell

10. Eddie Kendricks

11. Randy Crawford

12. Betty Wright

13. *The Poet*

14. The Temptations

15. The Ram Jam Band

SOUNDTRACKS

1. Melvin Van Peebles

2. *American Graffiti*

3. *Suspiria*

4. Ry Cooder

5. Ennio Morricone

6. The *Dirty Harry* series

7. *The Spy Who Loved Me*

8. BJ Thomas

9. *Against All Odds*

10. *One from the Heart*

11. James Brown

12. 'Everybody's Talkin''

13. *Performance*

14. 'Come And Get It'

15. Curtis Mayfield

SPACE SONGS

1. Barney Bubbles

2. Patti Smith

3. Sheila & B. Devotion

4. Can

5. The Slits

6. *The Yes Album*

7. *Feeling The Space*

8. Holland

9. Giorgio Moroder

10. 'Dark Star'

11. 'Vincent'

12. Parliament

13. 'No Doubt About It'

14. Rezillos

15. 'Magic Fly'

THE STONES' SECRETS

1. *Sticky Fingers*

2. *Tattoo You*

3. *Exile On Main St.*

4. *Black And Blue*

5. *Sticky Fingers*

6. *Black And Blue*

7. *Let It Bleed*

8. *Goats Head Soup*

9. *Black And Blue*

10. *Love You Live*

11. *Exile On Main St.*

12. *Black And Blue*

13. *Let It Bleed*

14. *Goats Head Soup*

15. *Tattoo You*

TEENAGE KICKS

1. Cockney Rebel
2. Flamin' Groovies
3. The Adverts
4. The Regents
5. The Sweet
6. Sonic Youth
7. David Bowie
8. Alice Cooper
9. Ramones
10. Marc Bolan & T. Rex
11. MC5
12. Buzzcocks
13. The Cramps
14. Eddie & The Hot Rods
15. Janis Ian

THAT'S MY RECORD!

1. Linda Ronstadt

2. Gregory Isaacs

3. Ratt

4. Frank Zappa

5. Roxy Music

6. ZZ Top

7. Santana

8. B-52's

9. King Crimson

10. Robert Palmer

11. Peter Hammill

12. Gil Scott-Heron

13. Hüsker Dü

14. Funkadelic

15. Talk Talk

THEY WROTE THE SONGS

1. Pete Ham and Tom Evans (Badfinger)

2. Curtis Mayfield

3. John Denver

4. Jeff Lynne

5. David Bowie

6. Paul McCartney and Michael Jackson

7. Prince

8. Leonard Cohen

9. Joni Mitchell

10. Morrissey & (Johnny) Marr

11. Elton John and Bernie Taupin

12. Ray Davies

13. Barry, Robin & Maurice Gibb (Bee Gees)

14. Stevie Wonder

15. Marc Bolan

TV

1. Keith Fordyce

2. Newcastle

3. Tony Wilson

4. *Colour Me Pop*

5. The Gojos

6. The Damned

7. Mike Nesmith

8. Alternative TV

9. A-Ha

10. Public Enemy

11. Don Henley

12. *Our World*

13. *Saturday Night Live*

14. The Adverts

15. Television

WEST COAST

1. 'Who Do You Love'

2. Barry Melton

3. *Clear Spot*

4. *Blows Against The Empire*

5. *Full Circle*

6. *Oar*

7. Ed Cassidy

8. Jorma Kaukonen

9. *Tales Of The Great Rum Runners*

10. Mickey Hart

11. Country Joe McDonald

12. The Full Tilt Boogie Band

13. Bryan MacLean

14. Moby Grape

15. Robby Krieger

WHISTLING SONGS

1. Otis Redding

2. John Lennon

3. The Lovin' Spoonful

4. Peter Gabriel

5. J. Geils Band

6. Captain Beefheart

7. Paul Simon

8. Guns N' Roses

9. David Bowie

10. The Beatles

11. Whistling Jack Smith

12. Scorpions

13. Billy Joel

14. Monty Python

15. Elton John

INTERLUDE

THE WHISTLE TEST TEST

1.   21 September 1971

2.   Nashville, Tennessee

3.   Michael Appleton

4.   *Whistle Test*

5.   *Time Out*

6.   *Melody Maker*

7.   A British Second World War RAF Commander

8.   Craig Chaquico

9.   Billy Bragg

10. *Sounds of the Seventies*

11. 1978

12. Anne Nightingale

13. Mark Ellen

14. Q

15. John Peel

THE BEST OF THE TEST?

1.   Jah Wobble

2.   *Roots*

3.   *Killer*

4.   'Next'

5.   Blue

6.   Patti Smith

7.   '(I'm Always Touched By Your) Presence, Dear'

8.   Roxy Music

9.   The Runaways

10.   *Unconditionally Guaranteed*

11.   *The End*

12.   Fred Neil

13.   Irmin Schmidt

14.   *Catch A Fire*

15.   Thijs van Leer

15 SONGS

1. Humble Pie

2. Iggy Pop

3. Lynyrd Skynyrd

4. Graham Nash

5. Television

6. Budgie

7. The Rezillos

8. Judee Sill

9. Linton Kwesi Johnson

10. Randy Newman

11. Aztec Camera

12. Elton John

13. XTC

14. Tom Waits

15. Cocteau Twins

WHO SAID WHAT?

1. The Adverts' TV Smith

2. Jerry Lee Lewis

3. XTC's Andy Partridge

4. The Jags

5. Robert Wyatt

6. Sad Café

7. Lynyrd Skynyrd's Ronnie van Zant

8. Ian Dury

9. Lemmy

10. Suggs from Madness

11. Kate Bush

12. Squeeze's Jools Holland

13. John Lennon

14. Wild Willy Barrett

15. Ivor Cutler

THE OGWT YEARS: 1971

1. Kris Kristofferson

2. Paris

3. 'Reason To Believe'

4. Morocco

5. Bill Graham

6. *Black Moses*

7. *200 Motels*

8. 'Double Barrel'

9. The Tams

10. Jonathan King

11. Carole King

12. Duane Allman

13. Little Feat

14. *Master Of Reality*

15. *Music*

THE OGWT YEARS: 1972

1. 'Debora'
2. Al Green
3. *Pink Moon*
4. Todd Rundgren
5. *Slade Alive!*
6. London
7. Barbet Schroeder
8. The White Panthers
9. David Gates
10. *Europe '72*
11. 'Frankenstein'
12. The Zombies
13. Wattstax
14. Danny Whitten
15. Asylum

THE OGWT YEARS: 1973

1.   Mickie Most

2.   *The Dark Side Of The Moon* (by Pink Floyd)

3.   *Tubular Bells* (by Mike Oldfield)

4.   Don Powell

5.   David Bowie

6.   Stealers Wheel

7.   The Byrds

8.   John Martyn

9.   Jefferson Airplane

10. *Pat Garrett & Billy The Kid*

11. 3

12. Roy Wood

13. 'Can The Can'

14. 'Nutbush City Limits'

15. *Never Turn Your Back On A Friend*

THE OGWT YEARS: 1974

1. 'Jumpin' Jack Flash'

2. Harry Nilsson

3. *Slaughter On 10th Avenue*

4. Ann Peebles

5. Marc Bolan

6. *Pretzel Logic*

7. Brighton

8. Supertramp

9. Philadelphia

10. Robert Wyatt

11. Ian Hunter

12. Elkie Brooks

13. Silverhead

14. Kenny Gamble and Leon Huff

15. 1967

THE OGWT YEARS: 1975

1. 'Cracked Actor'

2. Pete Ham

3. 'Miracles'

4. 'Cut The Cake'

5. The Four Seasons

6. Greg Lake

7. 'Jive Talkin''

8. Greg Allman

9. Jackie Wilson

10. 1968

11. Sweet

12. *On The Level*

13. Minnie Riperton

14. Canvey Island

15. 10cc

THE OGWT YEARS: 1976

1. 'Show Me The Way'

2. The Walker Brothers

3. David Byron

4. Rod Stewart

5. Florence Ballard

6. Fatback Band

7. Phil Ochs

8. Peter Tosh

9. The Raspberries

10. Jethro Tull

11. Lee 'Scratch' Perry

12. Bob Weir

13. Knebworth

14. Jerry Hall

15. John Miles

THE OGWT YEARS: 1977

1. Don Letts

2. Studio 54

3. 'God Save The Queen'

4. Ginger Alden

5. Robert Stigwood

6. Mick Jones

7. Hall & Oates

8. Steve Hackett

9. The Screen on the Green

10. Richard Lloyd

11. Gene Vincent

12. Marvin Gaye

13. Buzzcocks

14. Somerset

15. The Damned

THE OGWT YEARS: 1978

1. *Renaldo And Clara*

2. 'Jamming'

3. *Abbey Road*

4. Nancy Spungeon

5. Chaka Khan

6. Ordered to perform a benefit concert

7. Jello Biafra

8. *City To City*

9. Nick Lowe

10. The Rutles

11. Jacques Morali

12. *The Man-Machine*

13. Thin Lizzy

14. 'My Best Friend's Girl'

15. Talking Heads

THE OGWT YEARS: 1979

1. Ronnie James Dio

2. The Sugarhill Gang

3. M

4. Kenney Jones

5. Eddie 'Tenpole' Tudor

6. Supertramp

7. Rickie Lee Jones

8. *Euroman Cometh*

9. *Down On The Farm*

10. The New Barbarians

11. The Cure

12. The Slits

13. Sham 69

14. 'Whatever You Want'

15. 'He's The Greatest Dancer'

THE OGWT YEARS: 1980

1. John Lennon

2. Young Marble Giants

3. Biff Byford

4. Pete Townshend

5. *Crocodiles*

6. Dexys Midnight Runners

7. Siouxsie And The Banshees

8. Phil Lynott

9. Eddy Grant

10. The Burundi beat

11. Agnetha Faltskog

12. John Holt

13. Colossal Youth

14. Masturbation

15. Compass Point

THE OGWT YEARS: 1981

1. Generation X

2. Smokey Robinson

3. Finland

4. *My Life In The Bush Of Ghosts*

5. Quincy Jones

6. It is a 10" record

7. *Chariots of Fire*

8. Wendy O. Williams

9. John Lennon's bloodstained glasses

10. Marty Wilde

11. *Dangerous Acquaintances*

12. *Forever, Michael*

13. Lesley Gore

14. Cher

15. Bill Wyman

THE OGWT YEARS: 1982

1.   The Alamo

2.   David Byrne

3.   Jimmy Page

4.   Robert Quine

5.   'A Town Called Malice'

6.   Mick Jones

7.   *Still Life (American Concert 1981)*

8.   Smokey Robinson

9.   *Rocky III*

10. *Jump To It*

11. Iceland

12. Gary Numan

13. *Ice Cream For Crow*

14. Buffy Sainte-Marie and Jack Nitzsche

15. 'Cat People (Putting Out Fire)'

THE OGWT YEARS: 1983

1. *War*

2. David Crosby

3. The Immaculate Consumptive

4. Trevor Horn

5. Quiet Riot

6. Pulp

7. *Kill 'Em All*

8. *Everybody's Rockin'*

9. Godley & Creme

10. *Live In Tokyo*

11. Matt Johnson

12. Eddie Van Halen

13. Brixton

14. Paul Morley

15. Christie Brinkley

THE OGWT YEARS: 1984

1. Pepsi

2. 'In The Ghetto'

3. Renate Blauel

4. Cyndi Lauper

5. *Smell The Glove*

6. Sade

7. Nena

8. Wham!

9. Mick Fleetwood

10. Sandie Shaw

11. Tipper Gore

12. 'Hole In My Shoe'

13. North Wales

14. *About Face*

15. The Pointer Sisters

THE OGWT YEARS: 1985

1. Sammy Hagar

2. The Virgin Tour

3. Michael Jackson

4. Twisted Sister

5. The Minutemen

6. Run-D.M.C.

7. *VU*

8. Eric Clapton

9. *Bad Moon Rising*

10. Peter Gabriel

11. Robert Palmer

12. Freddie Mercury

13. Aretha Franklin

14. *Brothers In Arms*

15. Cameo

THE OGWT YEARS: 1986

1. *Menlove Ave.*

2. Beastie Boys

3. The Bangles

4. Chaka Khan

5. Cleveland, Ohio

6. Five

7. Def Jam

8. Bob & Earl

9. Sweden

10. Mike Rutherford

11. *Anything*

12. 'Wuthering Heights'

13. *London 0 Hull 4*

14. *Constrictor*

15. Eric B. & Rakim

THE OGWT YEARS: 1987

1.   T'Pau
2.   'You Keep Me Hangin' On'
3.   Dave Edmunds
4.   Public Enemy
5.   *Touch Of Grey*
6.   'Where The Streets Have No Name'
7.   Salt-N-Pepa
8.   Tommy James And The Shondells
9.   Ice-T
10.   *A Momentary Lapse Of Reason*
11.   Napalm Death
12.   'As Tears Go By'
13.   *Appetite For Destruction*
14.   *Hysteria*
15.   *The Glass Spider Tour*

SIDE B

ABBA

1.   1979
2.   1980
3.   1978
4.   1977
5.   1975
6.   1974
7.   1980
8.   1981
9.   1979
10. 1976
11. 1977
12. 1978
13. 1975
14. 1976
15. 1976

AC/DC

1. Malcolm Young

2. 'Rock 'n' Roll Damnation'

3. The Easybeats

4. 'All Because Of You'

5. *T.N.T.*

6. Glasgow

7. The Music Machine

8. Four

9. *For Those About To Rock We Salute You*

10. *Flick Of The Switch*

11. *Maximum Overdrive*

12. Scotland

13. Gibson SG

14. 'Rat Trap'

15. Little Richard

ALICE COOPER

1. Julie Covington

2. Kachina

3. Anthrax

4. *School's Out*

5. 'Reflected'

6. A preacher

7. Detroit

8. Bob Ezrin

9. John Lydon

10. 'Gutter Cat Vs. The Jets'

11. *Shocker*

12. Donovan

13. *Trash*

14. Dennis Dunaway

15. *Welcome To My Nightmare*

BAD COMPANY / FREE

1. Mick Ralphs

2. Back Street Crawler

3. King Crimson

4. Led Zeppelin

5. The Coasters

6. The Firm

7. Sharks

8. *Heartbreaker*

9. Guy Stevens

10. David Kossoff

11. 1973

12. *Free Live!*

13. The Doors

14. *Straight Shooter*

15. Brian Howe

THE BAND

1. 'Rag Mama Rag'
2. Joan Baez
3. *Moondog Matinee*
4. 'Georgia On My Mind'
5. 'Susie Q'
6. *Woodstock*
7. Julie Driscoll (with Adrian Edmondson)
8. 'The Weight'
9. Mickey Jones
10. West Saugerties
11. 'Sweet Fire Of Love'
12. Levon Helm
13. Eric Clapton
14. David Crosby
15. 1975

THE BEACH BOYS

1. 'Never Learn Not To Love'

2. Leonard Bernstein

3. The Students

4. Brother

5. Mike Love

6. Dean Torrence

7. *Stack-O-Tracks*

8. Hawthorne

9. 'Here Comes The Night'

10. A Chevrolet

11. Chynna Phillips

12. Marilyn Rovell

13. Eugene Landy

14. *Friends*

15. 'I Write The Songs'

THE BEATLES

1. 'Help!'

2. Aerosmith

3. The Residents

4. Ringo Starr (although a second version was recorded with session drummer Andy White)

5. 1965

6. Maureen Cleave

7. 'I Me Mine'

8. 'Get Back'

9. 'Dig It'

10. 'Sexy Sadie'

11. Marmalade

12. 1973

13. 1965

14. John Lennon

15. 'Within You Without You'

BEE GEES

1. 'Saved By The Bell'

2. Barry Gibb

3. *Cucumber Castle*

4. 'New York Mining Disaster 1941'

5. 'To Love Somebody'

6. 7

7. *Robin's Reign*

8. 'How Can You Mend A Broken Heart'

9. 'Chain Reaction'

10. Victoria Principal

11. 'Boom Bang-A-Bang'

12. Tavares

13. Peter Frampton

14. Robert Stigwood

15. *Odessa*

CHUCK BERRY

1. Keith Richards

2. Charles

3. 1963

4. 1979

5. The Duck Walk

6. *The London Chuck Berry Sessions*

7. The Steve Miller Band

8. *Concerto In B. Goode*

9. 'Roll Over Beethoven'

10. Spirit

11. 'Run Rudolph Run'

12. Johnnie Johnson

13. Berkeley Community Theatre, 30 May 1970

14. 'Sweet Little Sixteen'

15. Mike Douglas

BLACK SABBATH

1. Ronnie James Dio

2. Earth

3. 'N.I.B.'

4. Jethro Tull

5. Boris Karloff

6. Roger Bain

7. 'Never Say Die'

8. Don Arden

9. Blue Öyster Band

10. *Paranoid*

11. Lita Ford

12. Aimee

13. John Osbourne

14. Randy Rhoads

15. *Blizzard Of Ozz*

BLONDIE / DEBBIE HARRY

1. Private Stock

2. The Stilettos

3. Gary Valentine

4. 2

5. *KooKoo*

6. The Private Stock label

7. *Rockbird*

8. The Wind In The Willows

9. '(I'm Always Touched By Your) Presence, Dear'

10. Clem Burke

11. Randy & The Rainbows

12. 'Heart Of Glass'

13. 'Fade Away And Radiate'

14. *Call Me*

15. Nile Rodgers and Bernard Edwards

MARC BOLAN AND T. REX

1. 'Midsummer Night's Scene'

2. Hackney

3. *The Lord of the Rings*

4. Dib Cochran & The Earwigs

5. Eric Clapton

6. 'The Prettiest Star'

7. The Turtles

8. Rick Wakeman

9. Geoffrey Bayldon alias Catweazle

10. Cilla Black

11. 'Get It On'

12. John Peel

13. The Hidden Riders Of Tomorrow

14. 'To Know Him Is To Love Him' (retitled 'To Know You Is To Love You')

15. David Bowie

DAVID BOWIE

1. Elvis Presley

2. Sigma Sound Studios

3. Saxophone

4. *The Man Who Sold The World*

5. The Rats

6. Twiggy

7. *The 1980 Floor Show*

8. Thomas Jerome Newton

9. 'Space Oddity' (on its reissue in 1975)

10. Tony Visconti and Mary Hopkin

11. Hansa Studios

12. Joseph Merrick

13. Eddie Floyd

14. *Earthling*

15. Guy Peellaert

JAMES BROWN

1. *Live At The Apollo*

2. 'Papa's Got A Brand New Pigbag'

3. 'It's A Man's Man's Man's World'

4. 'Say It Loud – I'm Black And I'm Proud'

5. *The T.A.M.I. Show*

6. 1970

7. Bootsy Collins

8. 'Get Up (I Feel Like Being A) Sex Machine'

9. Richard Nixon

10. 'Cold Sweat'

11. George Foreman

12. *Rocky IV*

13. The Famous Flames

14. 2006

15. Carlos Alomar

KATE BUSH

1. *The Dreaming*

2. The KT Bush Band

3. 'Rocket Man'

4. David Gilmour

5. 'A Deal With God'

6. *Lionheart*

7. Paddy Bush

8. 1980's *Never For Ever*

9. 'No Self Control'

10. Delius

11. 1980

12. 'Running Up That Hill'

13. She toured

14. Moira Shearer

15. 'Come Together'

ERIC CLAPTON

1. *In Concert*

2. Japan

3. 'Badge'

4. Carl Radle

5. Pete Townshend

6. 'After Midnight'

7. Woman tone

8. 'Wonderful Tonight'

9. Ric Grech

10. The Dirty Mac

11. The Preacher

12. *Money And Cigarettes*

13. 'Little Wing'

14. Blackie

15. *We're Only In It For The Money* by the Mothers Of Invention

THE CLASH

1. Don Letts

2. Tory Crimes

3. 'Junco Partner'

4. Richard Dudanski

5. 'Complete Control'

6. A diplomat

7. *No. 10, Upping St.*

8. Subway Sect

9. Junior Murvin

10. Racing pigeons

11. Nicky Headon

12. Caroline Coon

13. Vince Taylor

14. The Bobby Fuller Four

15. A painter

LEONARD COHEN

1. 'Famous Blue Raincoat'

2. Hydra

3. *Beautiful Losers*

4. John Cale

5. Buffy Sainte-Marie

6. *From Her To Eternity*

7. The Army

8. *McCabe & Mrs Miller*

9. *Death Of A Ladies' Man*

10. *Songs From A Room*

11. *I'm Your Man*

12. Judy Collins

13. Kaleidoscope

14. 'Pennyroyal Tea'

15. Bob Johnston

ELVIS COSTELLO

1. Sam & Dave

2. *Armed Forces*

3. Nick Lowe

4. Napoleon Dynamite

5. The Pogues

6. The Joe Loss Orchestra

7. Jake Riviera

8. 'I Just Don't Know What To Do With Myself'

9. *Live At The El Mocambo*

10. 'Oliver's Army'

11. *Trust*

12. Bret Easton Ellis

13. George Jones

14. *King Of America*

15. 'Pills And Soap'

CROSBY, STILLS, NASH AND YOUNG

1. Stephen Stills

2. *What Goes Around*

3. 'Triad'

4. *Long May You Run*

5. A curfew on Sunset Strip

6. Poco

7. 'Marrakesh Express'

8. Judy Collins

9. Stephen Stills

10. Matthews' Southern Comfort

11. 'Southern Man'

12. 'Love The One You're With'

13. Manassas

14. 'I'm Alive'

15. 'Wasted On The Way'

MILES DAVIS

1. Teo Macero

2. *Sketches Of Spain*

3. Betty Davis

4. None

5. Chick Corea

6. Charlie Parker

7. John McLaughlin

8. *On The Corner*

9. *Amandla*

10. *You're Under Arrest*

11. A champion heavyweight boxer

12. Herbie Hancock

13. Darryl Jones

14. *Miami Vice*

15. Artists United Against Apartheid

DEEP PURPLE

1. The Mothers Of Invention

2. Elf

3. The James Gang

4. Mount Rushmore

5. Episode Six

6. Roger Glover

7. Joe Meek

8. Rod Evans

9. 'Hush'

10. 'Fireball'

11. 'Space Truckin''

12. Trapeze

13. Teaser

14. *Perfect Strangers*

15. Ian Gillan

BOB DYLAN

1. *The Freewheelin' Bob Dylan*

2. *Street Legal*

3. DA Pennebaker

4. *Nashville Skyline*

5. 'The Boxer'

6. Sam Peckinpah

7. Eric Clapton

8. The Wallflowers

9. 'Simple Twist Of Fate'

10. 'Hurricane'

11. *Street Legal*

12. 'Gotta Serve Somebody'

13. 'Blind Willie McTell'

14. *Biograph*

15. 'If Not For You'

THE EAGLES

1. Linda Ronstadt

2. Danny Kortchmar

3. Jackson Browne

4. The Flying Burrito Brothers

5. 'Best Of My Love'

6. *Desperado*

7. 'I Wish You Peace'

8. Timothy B. Schmit

9. The James Gang

10. The Beverly Hills Hotel on Sunset Boulevard, Los Angeles

11. *Little Criminals*

12. 'James Dean'

13. *Fast Times at Ridgemont High*

14. Glenn Frey

15. Don Henley

FLEETWOOD MAC

1. *Buckingham Nicks*

2. Four

3. 'Tusk'

4. Mick Taylor

5. Mike Vernon

6. 'Oh Well'

7. 'I'd Rather Go Blind'

8. *Bare Trees*

9. 'Albatross'

10. Bob Welch

11. Christine McVie

12. Stephanie

13. Wales

14. The Children of God

15. Mick Fleetwood

ARETHA FRANKLIN

1. 'Bridge Over Troubled Water'

2. Carolyn Franklin

3. Otis Redding

4. Four

5. Erma Franklin

6. Dionne Warwick

7. 'Think'

8. 'Jumpin' Jack Flash'

9. Cissy Houston

10. 'I Knew You Were Waiting (For Me)'

11. Eurythmics

12. Ben E. King

13. 'Amazing Grace'

14. Memphis, Tennessee

15. Jerry Wexler

MARVIN GAYE

1. 'What's Going On'

2. 'Sexual Healing'

3. Ostend, Belgium

4. Marvin Gay

5. 'The Onion Song'

6. Gladys Knight & The Pips

7. The Four Tops

8. *Trouble Man*

9. 'The Ecology'

10. 'Make Me Wanna Holler'

11. The Stylistics

12. Janis Hunter

13. Diana Ross

14. Nona Gaye

15. 'Sexual Healing'

GENESIS

1. *A Trick Of The Tail*

2. 1972

3. 'Puss 'n Boots'

4. Steve Biko

5. Charterhouse

6. 'Follow You Follow Me'

7. *Trespass*

8. *Nursery Cryme*

9. *Smallcreep's Day*

10. Polar Studios

11. Brand X

12. Tony Levin

13. *Selling England By The Pound*

14. Steve Hackett

15. Steve Howe

GEORGE HARRISON

1. Billy Preston

2. Todd Rundgren

3. Friar Park

4. Dark Horse

5. Splinter

6. 'Ding Dong, Ding Dong'

7. 'Don't Bother Me'

8. 'Norwegian Wood (This Bird Has Flown)'

9. 'He's So Fine' by the Chiffons

10. *Monty Python's Life Of Brian*

11. 'Govinda'

12. *Wonderwall*

13. Mick Fleetwood

14. 'Apple Scruffs'

15. James Ray

HAWKWIND / MOTÖRHEAD

1. 'Leaving Here'

2. *Space Ritual Alive*

3. Stacia

4. Ginger Baker

5. *Captain Lockheed And The Starfighters*

6. 'Silver Machine'

7. The creator of the band's light show

8. *In Search Of Space*

9. David Bowie

10. *St Valentine's Day Massacre*

11. Ian Kilmister

12. Inner City Unit

13. A Portobello Road café

14. Top 3

15. Eric Clapton

JIMI HENDRIX

1. The US Army (101st Airborne Division)

2. Jeff Beck

3. The Riot Squad

4. Marshall

5. 'Strangers In The Night'

6. Brian Jones

7. *Nine To The Universe*

8. 'Hey Joe'

9. Jack Casady

10. Fat Mattress

11. Rioting Hell's Angels

12. Monika Dannemann

13. Slade

14. Berkeley, California, 30 May 1970

15. Randy California

IRON MAIDEN

1. Paul Di'Anno

2. Rod Smallwood

3. Derek Riggs

4. 'Sanctuary'

5. Martin Birch

6. Samson

7. *The Number Of The Beast*

8. *The Soundhouse Tapes*

9. An instrument of torture

10. *Killers*

11. Edgar Allen Poe

12. 6, 6, and 6

13. No (it's Barry Clayton)

14. *Powerslave*

15. *Metal For Muthas*

MICHAEL JACKSON / JACKSON 5

1. Lionel Richie

2. 'I'll Be There'

3. Jackson Browne

4. Diana Ross

5. The Scarecrow

6. Quincy Jones

7. 'Rockin' Robin'

8. Less than two years

9. 'Say Say Say'

10. Heatwave

11. Vincent Price

12. 'Come Together'

13. *Victory*

14. 'One Day In Your Life'

15. 1986

JETHRO TULL

1. Jethro Toe

2. Glenn Cornick

3. *Thick As A Brick*

4. Barriemore Barlow

5. *A Passion Play*

6. *A*

7. Dave Pegg

8. Roland Kirk

9. *Now We Are Six*

10. Mick Abrahams

11. Curry

12. Martin Barre

13. *A Passion Play*

14. Salmon farms

15. Chrysalis

ELTON JOHN

1. *Honky Chateau*

2. *Too Low For Zero*

3. 'Philadelphia Freedom'

4. 'I Saw Her Standing There'

5. Lulu

6. Davey Johnstone

7. A recording studio outside Paris, the Chateau d'Herouville

8. Alice Cooper

9. 'Daniel'

10. Dr Winston O'Boogie

11. Kiki Dee

12. *Too Low For Zero*

13. 1969

14. George Michael

15. Saxon

JOY DIVISION / NEW ORDER

1. Warsaw

2. Before

3. Johnny Marr

4. 'Ceremony'

5. *Stroszek*

6. 'Blue Monday' (1988 Remix)

7. 'Transmission'

8. Sordide Sentimental

9. Stephen Morris

10. *Touching from a Distance: Ian Curtis and Joy Division*

11. 'Blue Monday'

12. 'Sister Ray'

13. Rob Gretton

14. *So It Goes*

15. *Closer*

THE KINKS

1. Rasa

2. Muswell Hill

3. Cardiff

4. 'All Day And All Of The Night'

5. 'See My Friends'

6. *The Kinks Are The Village Green Preservation Society*

7. *Lola Versus Powerman And The Moneygoround, Part One*

8. Konk

9. Mr Flash

10. The Pretenders

11. 'Sunny Afternoon'

12. 'Come Dancing'

13. *Return to Waterloo*

14. 'Susannah's Still Alive'

15. Shel Talmy

KISS

1. Paul Stanley

2. Hello

3. Casablanca

4. Bob Ezrin

5. 1980

6. Vinnie Vincent

7. 'Do You Love Me?'

8. Gene Simmons

9. *Kiss Meets The Phantom Of The Park*

10. Peter Criss

11. *Lick It Up*

12. Ace Frehley

13. 'Rock 'n' Roll All Nite'

14. 'Then He Kissed Me'

15. Paul Stanley

LED ZEPPELIN

1. Giant's Causeway

2. Kenneth Anger

3. Swan Song Records

4. *Silk Torpedo*

5. Band Of Joy

6. PJ Proby

7. Peter Grant

8. 'Dazed And Confused'

9. 'Moby Dick'

10. Bron-Yr-Aur

11. 'The Battle Of Evermore'

12. Madison Square Garden

13. The Starship

14. *In Through The Out Door*

15. The Honeydrippers

JOHN LENNON

1. Hot Chocolate (as Hot Chocolate Band)

2. Arthur Janov

3. Sissy Spacek

4. 1952

5. *How I Won The War*

6. *No One's Gonna Change Our World*

7. *The Lives of John Lennon*

8. 'Gimme Some Truth'

9. Cheap Trick

10. Tony Visconti

11. 35th

12. Petula Clark

13. Acorns

14. 'Ya Ya'

15. *Mind Games*

MADONNA

1. The Breakfast Club
2. *The Who's That Girl World Tour*
3. *True Blue*
4. Michigan
5. Patrick Hernandez
6. 'Into The Groove'
7. Sonic Youth
8. 'Live To Tell'
9. 'Everybody'
10. The Beastie Boys
11. George Harrison
12. Her 1983 debut, *Madonna*
13. 'La Isla Bonita'
14. *The Who's That Girl World Tour*
15. 'Borderline'

BOB MARLEY & THE WAILERS

1. Bunny Wailer

2. *Catch A Fire*

3. Tuff Gong

4. The I Threes

5. The Smile Jamaica Concert

6. 'People Get Ready'

7. Rhodesia

8. *Burnin'*

9. 'Punky Reggae Party'

10. Clement 'Coxsone' Dodd

11. The Lyceum Ballroom

12. Peter Tosh

13. Aston Barrett

14. 'Stir It Up'

15. Lee 'Scratch' Perry

PAUL McCARTNEY

1. 'Girls' School'

2. Mary Hopkin

3. The National Trust

4. Denny Seiwell

5. *Ram*

6. 'C Moon'

7. Suzy And The Red Stripes

8. Thunderclap Newman

9. 'Give Ireland Back To The Irish' by Wings

10. Hofner

11. A dog

12. Lagos, Nigeria

13. David Gilmour

14. *Press To Play*

15. Eric Stewart

JONI MITCHELL

1. Buffy Sainte-Marie

2. Roberta Joan Anderson

3. Judy Collins

4. 'Big Yellow Taxi'

5. 'This Flight Tonight'

6. Thomas Dolby

7. Jaco Pastorius

8. *Court And Spark*

9. *Clouds*

10. Charles Mingus

11. *For The Roses*

12. David Crosby

13. Laurel Canyon

14. 1975

15. Journey

VAN MORRISON

1. 'Here Comes The Night'

2. *Blowin' Your Mind!*

3. 'Jackie Wilson Said (I'm In Heaven When You Smile)'

4. 'Gloria'

5. *No Guru, No Method, No Teacher*

6. John Lee Hooker

7. Them

8. 1968

9. *His Band And The Street Choir*

10. *A Period Of Transition*

11. 'Caravan'

12. George Ivan Morrison

13. Janet Planet

14. The Caledonia Soul Orchestra

15. *It's Too Late To Stop Now*

NEW YORK DOLLS

1. 'Jet Boy'

2. Barbara Hulanicki

3. Steven Morrissey

4. Shadow Morton

5. Blackie Lawless

6. *L.A.M.F.*

7. Jerry Nolan

8. Sylvain Sylvain

9. Killer

10. Communist hammer 'n' sickle

11. *Red Patent Leather*

12. The Kinks

13. Richard Hell And The Voidoids

14. David Johansen

15. The Foundations

PINK FLOYD

1. Ron Geesin

2. *A Bizarre Collection Of Antiques & Curios*

3. Jokers Wild

4. Jenny Spires

5. 'Oh Babe What Would You Say?'

6. Soft Machine

7. Steve Marriott

8. 'Come In Number 51, Your Time Is Up'

9. Clare Torry

10. 'Sheep'

11. Montreal

12. Nick Mason

13. Zee

14. *The Pros And Cons Of Hitch Hiking*

15. Hipgnosis

THE POLICE

1. Curved Air

2. 'I'll Be Missing You'

3. He was spotted wearing a yellow and black hooped shirt

4. *Ghost In The Machine*

5. Arthur Koestler

6. Henry Padovani

7. Miles Copeland

8. 'Message In A Bottle'

9. 'Don't Stand So Close To Me'

10. Nigel Gray

11. Ace Face

12. *Dune*

13. *The Dream Of The Blue Turtles*

14. Andy Summers

15. Stewart Copeland

IGGY POP / THE STOOGES

1. Scott Asheton

2. James (Newell) Osterberg

3. He once played in the group called the Iguanas

4. 'No Fun'

5. James Williamson

6. *Metallic KO*

7. 'Real Wild Child'

8. *The Idiot*

9. Siouxsie And The Banshees

10. Glen Matlock

11. Steve Jones

12. The Psychedelic Stooges

13. Danny Fields

14. Ron Asheton

15. John Cale

ELVIS PRESLEY

1. 1969

2. *From Elvis In Memphis*

3. 'If I Can Dream'

4. 'Can't Help Falling In Love'

5. The International Hotel

6. Bill Belew

7. JD Sumner

8. James Burton

9. Dr Nick

10. The Memphis Mafia

11. *Elvis: What Happened?*

12. 'Way Down'

13. 'Are You Lonesome Tonight?'

14. 1973

15. Karate

PRINCE

1. 1982

2. Prince Rogers Nelson

3. Madonna

4. *For You*

5. Minneapolis, Minnesota

6. Sheila E.

7. *Under The Cherry Moon*

8. *Parade*

9. Sheena Easton

10. Wendy & Lisa

11. 'When Doves Cry'

12. The Time

13. 'Manic Monday'

14. The Family

15. 'Controversy'

QUEEN

1. 1975

2. Ealing Art College

3. Smile

4. Roger Taylor

5. Zanzibar

6. 'Keep Yourself Alive'

7. 'Under Pressure', a collaboration with David Bowie

8. Roger Taylor

9. *Jazz*

10. 'Bicycle Race'

11. Red Special

12. *News Of The World*

13. *Flash Gordon*

14. *Live Killers*

15. *Metropolis*

LOU REED / THE VELVET UNDERGROUND

1. With feedback and guitar effects

2. *Transformer*

3. *White Light/White Heat*

4. 'Heroin'

5. *Music For A New Society*

6. The Factory

7. Jackie Curtis

8. A whip

9. Terry Riley

10. Robert Quine

11. *Rock 'n' Roll Animal*

12. Kevin Ayers

13. *VU*

14. Both

15. 1993

R.E.M.

1. 'Radio Free Europe'

2. Joe Boyd

3. *Dead Letter Office*

4. 1985

5. 10,000 Maniacs

6. *Chronic Town*

7. *Document*

8. Bill Berry

9. Wire

10. Hindu Love Gods

11. 'The One I Love'

12. Athens, Georgia

13. Aerosmith

14. The Golden Palominos

15. 1988

THE ROLLING STONES

1. A.A. Milne

2. Merry Clayton

3. Michele Breton

4. The *Mandrax*

5. 'Time Waits For No One'

6. *Monkey Grip*

7. 'I Don't Know Why'

8. Charlie Watts

9. The Birds

10. Eric Donaldson

11. Sugar Blue

12. *Dirty Work*

13. 1985

14. 'C'mon, you little shower of shit'

15. Canned Heat

DIANA ROSS

1. *Lady Sings the Blues*

2. 1967

3. Marvin Gaye

4. 'Someday We'll Be Together'

5. *Everything Is Everything*

6. 'Theme From *Mahogany* (Do You Know Where You're Going To)'

7. *The Boss*

8. *diana*

9. *Endless Love*

10. (Nick) Ashford and (Valerie) Simpson

11. *Eaten Alive*

12. *An Evening With Diana Ross*

13. RCA

14. Jackson 5

15. 'Reach Out And Touch (Somebody's Hand)'

ROXY MUSIC AND ENO

1. 'Jealous Guy'

2. *Country Life*

3. Portsmouth Sinfonia

4. 'Do The Strand'

5. *In Search Of Eddie Riff*

6. Davy O'List

7. Curved Air

8. EG Management

9. 'Pyjamarama'

10. Antony Price

11. *Stranded*

12. *Let's Stick Together*

13. The Big Three / The Merseybeats

14. *Siren*

15. *Flesh And Blood*

SANTANA

1. *Moonflower*

2. *Love Devotion Surrender*

3. Journey

4. 'Soul Sacrifice'

5. Peter Green

6. 'Samba Pa Ti'

7. *Borboletta*

8. Alice Coltrane

9. *Havana Moon*

10. San Francisco

11. 'Evil Ways'

12. Tito Puente

13. Buddy Miles

14. *Caravanserai*

15. Sri Chinmoy

SEX PISTOLS

1. Television Personalities

2. Situationism

3. Rod Stewart's 'I Don't Want To Talk About It'

4. Too Fast To Live Too Young To Die

5. Hampstead

6. Flowers Of Romance

7. 'Understanding'

8. Chris Spedding

9. Van Der Graaf Generator

10. Sex Pistols On Tour Secretly

11. *Spunk*

12. *Ghosts Of Princes In Towers*

13. 'Friggin' In The Riggin''

14. *Some Product – Carri On Sex Pistols*

15. The Professionals

SIOUXSIE AND THE BANSHEES

1. *Captain Scarlet*

2. The Models / Rema-Rema

3. Bromley

4. Magazine

5. *Through The Looking Glass*

6. *Join Hands*

7. 'Spellbound'

8. *Hyaena*

9. The Glove

10. Ben E. King

11. Big In Japan

12. Altered Images

13. John 'Valentine' Carruthers

14. Julie Driscoll, Brian Auger and the Trinity

15. Kenny Morris

SLY AND THE FAMILY STONE

1. The Great Society

2. Magazine

3. *High On You*

4. Sly's sister Rose

5. Sylvester Stewart

6. Larry Graham

7. 'Everyday People'

8. 'Running Away'

9. 'Que Sera, Sera (Whatever Will Be, Will Be)'

10. Freddie Stone

11. None

12. On stage at Madison Square Garden in New York

13. 'Dance To The Music'

14. *Stand!*

15. Funkadelic

PATTI SMITH

1. 'Hey Joe'

2. *Nuggets: Original Artyfacts From The First Psychedelic Era 1965–1968*

3. Jimi Hendrix

4. The Stranglers

5. 'Time Is On My Side'

6. John Lennon

7. Electric Lady Studios

8. Half Japanese

9. Sam Shepard

10. Blue Oyster Cult

11. Patty Hearst

12. Fred 'Sonic' Smith

13. *Privilege*

14. *Seventh Heaven*

15. *Dream Of Life*

THE SMITHS

1. 'Heaven Knows I'm Miserable Now'

2. Viv Nicholson

3. Rough Trade

4. Billy Duffy

5. Buzzcocks drummer John Maher

6. Craig Gannon

7. Playwright Shelagh Delaney

8. 1986

9. Billy Fury

10. Vini Reilly

11. T. Rex

12. James Dean

13. *Orphée*

14. 'Shakespeare's Sister'

15. *The Queen Is Dead*

BRUCE SPRINGSTEEN

1. *Born To Run*

2. *Nebraska*

3. Clarence Clemons

4. Max Weinberg

5. Steven Van Zant

6. Patti Scialfa

7. John Hammond

8. *Born In The USA*

9. Courteney Cox

10. 'Hungry Heart'

11. *Rolling Stone*

12. Nils Lofgren

13. Hammersmith Odeon

14. 'Fire'

15. Chuck Berry

RINGO STARR

1. Johnny Burnette

2. 'I'm a Mocker.'

3. 'Octopus's Garden'

4. Pete Best

5. Jimmy Nicol

6. *Thomas the Tank Engine and Friends*

7. 'Good Night'

8. *Sentimental Journey*

9. George Harrison

10. *Caveman*

11. Billy Fury

12. 'It Don't Come Easy'

13. *Born To Boogie*

14. 'Back Off Boogaloo'

15. 'I'm The Greatest'

ROD STEWART / THE FACES

1. *The Cry Of Love*

2. The Sutherland Brothers Band

3. Tetsu Yamauchi

4. 'Street Fighting Man'

5. Highgate

6. Humble Pie

7. 'Reason To Believe'

8. The Isley Brothers

9. Ray Jackson

10. *A Nod Is As Good As A Wink... To A Blind Horse*

11. Ronnie Lane

12. 'You Wear It Well'

13. Steampacket

14. 'Baby Jane'

15. *Ooh La La*

10cc

1. 'Neanderthal Man'

2. 'For Your Love'

3. 'I Wish You Would'

4. The Mindbenders

5. Strawberry Studios

6. Lol Creme

7. Eric Stewart and Graham Gouldman

8. 'Dreadlock Holiday'

9. *Sheet Music*

10. 1976

11. 'Prince Charming'

12. Jonathan King

13. *How Dare You!*

14. The Gizmo, also known as the Gizmotron

15. Graham Gouldman

TRAFFIC

1. Dave Mason

2. Berkshire

3. *When The Eagle Flies*

4. *Back In The High Life*

5. *Here We Go Round the Mulberry Bush*

6. 'Keep On Running'

7. 'Feelin' Alright'

8. *On The Road*

9. *John Barleycorn Must Die*

10. Muff (or Mervyn) Winwood

11. Dave Mason

12. *Mr Fantasy*

13. Dave Mason

14. Jim Capaldi

15. *With Their New Face On*

U2

1. 'Pride (In The Name Of Love)'

2. David Evans

3. '11 O'Clock Tick Tock'

4. Paul McGuinness

5. 'Out Of Control'

6. *Under A Blood Red Sky*

7. Robbie Robertson

8. *The Unforgettable Fire*

9. *War*

10. Virgin Prunes

11. Paul Hewson

12. *Captive*

13. Windmill Lane Studios

14. 'Desire'

15. California

PAUL WELLER / THE JAM

1. *Something Else*

2. 'In The City'

3. Larry Williams

4. The Merton Parkas

5. 'A Town Called Malice'

6. Stiff Little Fingers

7. 'Going Underground'

8. Brighton

9. DC Lee

10. 'Soul Deep'

11. *Modernism: A New Decade*

12. *Our Favourite Shop*

13. Tracie

14. *My Ever Changing Moods*

15. *Snap!*

THE WHO

1. The Railway Hotel

2. The Beachcombers

3. Fontana

4. Constant Lambert / Terence Stamp

5. 'Happy Jack'

6. 'Down In The Tube Station At Midnight'

7. Woodstock Festival

8. The Priest

9. '5:15'

10. 'You Better You Bet'

11. Stargroves

12. Walker

13. John Entwistle

14. Keith Moon

15. *Who's Next*

STEVIE WONDER

1. Tonto's Expanding Head Band

2. Duke Ellington

3. 'Master Blaster (Jammin')'

4. 'Pastime Paradise'

5. Jeff Beck

6. 'I Just Called To Say I Love You'

7. *The Woman In Red*

8. 'Happy Birthday'

9. Michigan

10. The clavinet

11. 'You Are The Sunshine Of My Life'

12. 1973

13. 'Isn't She Lovely?'

14. *Characters*

15. *Where I'm Coming From*

NEIL YOUNG

1. *Trans*

2. 1966

3. *After The Gold Rush*

4. *Live Rust*

5. 'Revolution Blues'

6. Danny Whitten

7. Toronto

8. *Buffalo Springfield Again*

9. *Trans*

10. Elliot Roberts

11. *After The Gold Rush*

12. 1973

13. 'Cortez The Killer'

14. *Old Ways*

15. *Harvest*

ZAPPA / BEEFHEART

1. Don Glen Vliet

2. Eric Clapton

3. 'Willie The Pimp'

4. 'The Blimp'

5. 'Circle'

6. Cal Schenkel

7. Ian Underwood

8. Theodore Bikel

9. Jack Bruce

10. *Bluejeans & Moonbeams*

11. Alternative TV

12. Eric Drew Feldman

13. Parents Music Resource Center (PMRC)

14. Matt Groening

15. The Raspberries

BONUS TRACKS

TRACK 01

1. The Animals

2. Glen Campbell

3. Denny Laine

4. Clyde Stubblefield

5. Perrey and Kingsley

6. White Noise

7. Ian Hunter

8. Because his girlfriend Nancy Spungeon was found dead in their New York hotel room

9. Altamont

10. *The Harder They Come*

11. CBGB's

12. The Reclines

13. *Atlantic Crossing*

14. *Miniatures*

15. *Hail! Hail! Rock 'n' Roll*

TRACK 02

1. 1984

2. Warren Zevon

3. 'Power To The People'

4. Johnny Mathis and Deniece Williams

5. Ron Wood

6. The Fall

7. Nanci Griffith

8. *Young Americans*

9. 'Come Together'

10. Postcard Records

11. 'Something'

12. *Time Of No Reply*

13. *Look At The Fool*

14. AJ Weberman

15. 'Here Comes The Sun'

TRACK 03

1. *No Pussyfooting*

2. Johnny Paycheck

3. Billy Swan

4. Holger Czukay

5. The Eagles

6. 'Wild Horses'

7. Wings

8. Cher

9. Randy Bachman

10. Basildon

11. 'Blockbuster'

12. Mott The Hoople

13. 'Saturday Night'

14. Steve Miller

15. 'Can't Keep It In'

TRACK 04

1. 'The Butterfly Collector'

2. 'Anarchy In The UK'

3. Prince Buster

4. Ohio

5. Hylda Baker and Arthur Mullard

6. Elvis Costello

7. Poison Girls

8. Patti Smith

9. Joe Strummer

10. Donny Hathaway

11. *Tin Drum*

12. David Freiberg

13. Grateful Dead

14. John Entwistle

15. *Lie*

TRACK 05

1. Fine Young Cannibals
2. Dead Kennedys
3. The Chateau Marmont Hotel
4. Cabaret Voltaire
5. Curtis Mayfield
6. Swell Maps
7. Robert Freeman
8. Pink Military
9. Memphis Slim
10. Afrika Bambaataa
11. 1970
12. Lee Perry
13. UB40
14. Martin Hannett
15. Steve Lillywhite

TRACK 06

1. The Grease Band

2. Julie Driscoll

3. Aretha Franklin

4. Nile Rodgers

5. Mott The Hoople

6. *Touch*

7. Bob Dylan

8. HR Giger

9. Barry White

10. Robert Crumb

11. 1979

12. *Reproduction*

13. Billy Preston

14. Joy Division

15. Deadheads

TRACK 07

1. Elkie Brooks

2. Ring O'Records

3. 'They're Coming To Take Me Away, Ha-Haaa!'

4. Charles Manson

5. 'Son Of My Father'

6. The Finsbury Park Astoria

7. *Raft of the Medusa*

8. George O'Dowd

9. 'I Love To Love'

10. The Raspberries

11. 1974

12. Fleetwood Mac

13. Ginger Baker's Air Force

14. *A Collection Of Beatles Oldies (But Goldies!)*

15. Butthole Surfers

TRACK 08

1. *You Scare Me To Death*

2. Cabaret Voltaire

3. The Bible / Samuel Beckett

4. *Streetwalkers*

5. Girls Together Outrageously

6. Pentangle

7. The Slits

8. The Soft Machine

9. Donna Summer

10. 'What!'

11. 'Coup'

12. *154*

13. X-Ray Spex

14. *Decade*

15. *Bongo Fury*

TRACK 09

1. Petula Clark

2. Dave Swarbrick

3. *Amazing Grace*

4. Hammersmith Odeon, London

5. George Clinton

6. Moonwalk

7. Martin Degville

8. Chris Watson

9. Human League

10. Pete Shelley

11. Wings

12. William Burroughs

13. 'The Ballad Of John And Yoko'

14. Steve Albini

15. The Fall

TRACK 10

1. *Lotus*

2. Penetration

3. 'One And One Is One' / 'Rising Sun'

4. Butch Trucks

5. *Saint Dominic's Preview*

6. Todd Rundgren

7. Thin Lizzy

8. Boston

9. Robin Guthrie

10. *The World Is A Ghetto*

11. Fela Kuti

12. SST Records

13. The Smiths

14. Rock 'n' roll

15. 1985